T0277214

# NONLINEAR

**SIMPLICITY: DESIGN, TECHNOLOGY, BUSINESS, LIFE**

John Maeda, Editor

*The Laws of Simplicity*, John Maeda, 2006

*The Plenitude: Creativity, Innovation, and Making Stuff*, Rich Gold, 2007

*Simulation and Its Discontents*, Sherry Turkle, 2009

*Redesigning Leadership*, John Maeda, 2011

*I'll Have What She's Having*, Alex Bentley, Mark Earls, and Michael J. O'Brien, 2011

*The Storm of Creativity*, Kyna Leski, 2015

*The Acceleration of Cultural Change: From Ancestors to Algorithms*, R. Alexander Bentley and Michael J. O'Brien, 2017

*Mismatch*, Kat Holmes, 2018

*The Importance of Small Decisions: How Culture Evolves*, Michael J. O'Brien, R. Alexander Bentley, and William A. Brock, 2019

*Reimagining Design: Unlocking Strategic Innovation*, Kevin G. Bethune, 2022

*Nonlinear: Navigating Design with Curiosity and Conviction*, Kevin G. Bethune, 2025

# NONLINEAR

## Navigating Design with Curiosity and Conviction

### KEVIN G. BETHUNE

#### FOREWORD BY JOHN MAEDA

The MIT Press
Cambridge, Massachusetts
London, England

The MIT Press would like to thank the anonymous peer reviewers who provided comments on drafts of this book. The generous work of academic experts is essential for establishing the authority and quality of our publications. We acknowledge with gratitude the contributions of these otherwise uncredited readers.

This book was set in Scala and Scala Sans by New Best-set Typesetters Ltd. Printed and bound in the United States of America.

Library of Congress Cataloging-in-Publication Data

Names: Bethune, Kevin G., author. | Maeda, John, writer of foreword.
Title: Nonlinear : navigating design with curiosity and conviction /
    Kevin G. Bethune ; foreword by John Maeda.
Description: Cambridge, Massachusetts : The MIT Press, [2025] | Series:
    Simplicity: design, technology, business, life | Includes bibliographical
    references and index.
Identifiers: LCCN 2024017259 (print) | LCCN 2024017260 (ebook) |
    ISBN 9780262049436 (hardcover) | ISBN 9780262381284 (epub) |
    ISBN 9780262381291 (pdf)
Subjects: LCSH: Design—Social aspects.
Classification: LCC NK1520 .B49 2025 (print) | LCC NK1520 (ebook) |
    DDC 620.8/2—dc23/eng/20240826
LC record available at https://lccn.loc.gov/2024017259
LC ebook record available at https://lccn.loc.gov/2024017260

10  9  8  7  6  5  4  3  2  1

For Sefanit and Ezra.

For Lonnie, Beverly, Travis, and Serene.

For my circle of family, friends, mentors, and encouragers.

Thank you for your steadfast love and support.

Now faith is the substance of things hoped for, the evidence of things not seen.

—Hebrews 11:1

# CONTENTS

I once found myself between flights in Los Angeles, driving around the airport in Kevin's car. The world outside was moving at jet speed, much like our conversation within. It was a fleeting moment between cities, yet in those minutes, we traversed the breadth of his book *Reimagining Design: Unlocking Strategic Innovation*. That drive was a physical echo of the journey through his thoughts—a prelude to this very moment where *Nonlinear: Navigating Design with Curiosity and Conviction* beckons us toward a new horizon.

Kevin has a rare gift: he frames the quantitative with an artist's touch and delves into the qualitative with a scientist's eye. Through Kevin's many lenses, or "looking glasses," as he likes to call them, I have seen the world not as a series of discrete points, but as a continuous narrative—a tapestry woven with threads of data and genuine human moments. His new work is a testament to this vision, a guide that navigates the vastness of design with the precision of an experienced cartographer and the wisdom of a humble sage.

As we drove, the conversation deepened, mirroring the layers that Kevin has peeled back in his lifetime pursuit of relevant innovation. Our dialogue, though brief, was a dance of ideas, each step leading seamlessly to the next. This book is a partner to that dance, inviting us to step into the rhythm of Kevin's thoughts, to feel the pulse of his lived experience. There is not a moment throughout the book when you ever feel like you've stepped on Kevin's toes. In fact, he welcomes you onto the dance floor to experiment to your fullest without any judgment.

*Nonlinear* is a necessary bridge between worlds, a pathway for the designer to gain MBA acumen and for the strategist to master the craft of design. It is an invitation to cross the river of convention, to blend the analytical with the creative, and in doing so, to become fluent in both languages. There is no better book at this moment, when the prophecy of AI's eventual domination can be countered by sheer human will born of intuition, foresight, and love—qualities that Kevin has arduously encoded for us all.

Within these seemingly linear pages of *Nonlinear* lies the cross-pollination of disciplines—a journey as pivotal for the seasoned designer as it is for the business strategist. It is a zigzagging, brain-busting blueprint for those who dare to wear both hats—for the artist who seeks the logic of the market, and for the executive who yearns to harness the power of design thinking.

As a friend, as an admirer, I am moved by Kevin's unwavering commitment to the transformative power of design. His words are an important beacon, guiding us through the intricacies of innovation with warmth and undeniable sincerity. I feel lucky to know such a special person, and I feel fortunate for you to learn more about this magical mind that the world needs now more than ever.

Our drive around LAX eventually ended as I needed to catch my next plane, but the journey did not. With *Nonlinear*, I feel that we continue to travel along Kevin's extraordinary path. Each page is a step, each chapter a mile, each concept a destination. Join us on this venture—a voyage not just through design, but through the very fabric of creative thought. And don't worry: you're certain to still make your next flight, thanks to the brevity of his prose, by design.

—John Maeda, creativeleadership.com

# 1 ZIG THEN ZAG

LIFE IS A NONLINEAR JOURNEY.

I am a product of a very windy road. I am a designer, entrepreneur, and author based in Redondo Beach, California. I am a husband, a father, and a Black man who's navigated a very unique journey of multidisciplinary leaps. I am a descendent of America's original sin of chattel slavery, continually imagining the strength and resilience that embodied my ancestors' experience. I am married to an Ethiopian-born American who is more able to trace her history as far back as three thousand years from the days of King Menelik and Queen Sheba. Our teenage son represents an amalgamation of both threads of histories and cultures. He lives in a world still plagued by the threads of systemic inequity that attempt to convince him that he's "less than" or an "other" based purely on the color of his skin. We do our best to expose him to as many things as possible so that he begins to imagine himself doing great things in the future. His dreams matter. We believe in his potential. I try not to worry as he navigates a world vulnerable to police brutality and schools unsafe from guns. I have to place my faith in God for his safety and the safety of my family. Part of recognizing who I am, and who the folks I'm representing are, is that I will consciously rebel against the challenges we face with hope, faith, optimism, curiosity, and creativity. *I am.*

At the same time, I should embrace another human being with equal gravity. *They are. You are.* There is the full breadth and depth of a person's humanity that we should acknowledge and respect. We need to engage others with complete humility, empathy, and compassion. We are not the same, and that's a beautiful thing. Our stories are like fingerprints: very different. Yours is no more worthy than mine, and vice versa. However, our reverence for each other should hold enough weight to spark healthy curiosity and empathy for one another. In doing so, we'll unearth opportunities to see the common threads that lie between us, and we'll share in a common purpose. We can do that while celebrating what makes us different. We should celebrate what we can learn about each other. At the same time, we should also recognize that we navigate much of the same world, the same spaces, and the same constructs. Aspects of my story may not directly translate to someone else, but we might identify with the same circumstances. You might be a parent, the same as me. Despite living in different cities, we may be wresting with remote work through Zoom calls and Slack threads. We can be different and similar, at the same time. When sharing from my lived experiences, I am careful to say that I can only speak for me. Just because I experience something, I shouldn't assume the same reality on you. I don't want anyone to feel like they have to do exactly what I've done. My only hope is that you might use my story as a mirror to see yourself a little differently and find the courage to bring your full humanity to everything you do.

As we think about how we journey forward in life, the spaces and structures that we navigate are the way they are by design. They were informed by someone. When given an opportunity, we have to unravel who was actually at the table in informing these constructs and recognize the threads of systemic inequity that have persisted within them. My first book, *Reimagining Design: Unlocking Strategic Innovation,* shined a light on the importance of design at parity with other disciplines in informing the evolution of our spaces, enterprises, and institutions with the hope that we can inform better futures. I wrote it for anyone (regardless of discipline) who's creatively curious and likely to be proximate to design within a multidisciplinary team. I wrote it for those who wondering how to position themselves in a world undergoing multidisciplinary convergence to meet the complex challenges of our time, and to help them figure out how to make lasting, positive change. For design in particular, I find that designers are especially passionate about the human condition. Their arrival at the problem-solving table is surely welcome based on what the world desperately needs right now—more empathy and compassion. At the same time, their arrival runs in the face of predominant forces that have shaped industries as we know them. From business titans who set the tone of Wall Street to Silicon Valley technologists who pioneered the digitization of our world, design has an opportunity to set a new precedent, a new tone. These precedents are important as we think about bringing the right people around the table.

As we look forward, we can't forget the underlying thread of diversity, equity, and inclusion (DEI) to ensure the mix of folks around the table actually mirrors the world in terms of representation. Far too many self-proclaimed "world-class" brands and organizations claim to "design for" or "build for" their customers. However, when you peer inside their hallways, their team composition fails to reflect the beautiful diversity of our society. It's even worse when it comes to their leadership pipelines and board rooms. They will claim rightful position based on a shaky premise of meritocracy and how they ascended career ladders of hardened pedigree. Considering the threads of systemic inequity and the paradigms of power and privilege, is it really that simple? Does it explain why so many are left out? Upon examining their understanding of customers and stakeholders, we usually find significant amounts of bias and blind spots between their offerings and what people actually need. These issues could be avoided if they respected their audience with humility and brought them into the process (i.e., if they opted to design *with* or build *with*). I will boldly say that we need to go even further. Beyond *designing with*, we need to ensure our teams actually include representative members of our diverse society. Representative teammates could broker authentic inroads into those communities that we have yet to authentically engage. Within design, I find the low percentage of BIPOC (Black, Indigenous, people of color) professionals especially disappointing. Our future teams should mirror the beautiful tapestry that is the world.

Even if a team is multidisciplinary and more diverse by representation, I've learned that who's at the table isn't enough. How that team actually navigates through the work is extremely important too. We have to think about what we expect a multidisciplinary, diverse team to do when facing any opportunity to create something new. Each person brings their own perspective, behaviors, language, and skillsets. Even starting with the basic question of "Who should lead?" opens the door for all kinds of baggage to be revealed. If we remember the dominant precedents that inform the status quo for most organizations, we'll quickly realize the existence of biases as it relates to leadership tact, collaboration behavior, and the exchange of what people ultimately value. When we think about the disciplines around the table, certain individuals might quickly snap into a particular way of doing things and expect others to follow suit. Depending on the level of political capital around that table, some disciplines may immediately get their way while others are quickly subordinated, sometimes without knowing it. This can resemble an expected march of expectations: I do this, then you do that. Once you're done, I expect you to pass that output along to the next person and she does this, and so on. Over time, these transactional behaviors start to harden and become engrained in the company's way of doing things. It becomes the precedent.

This dilemma grows the bigger a company becomes. Any new approach is usually met with skepticism. Any technique that slows down the cadence of problem-solving might be viewed as heresy. More than likely, departments would rather lean into their proven and tested playbooks under most circumstances. Playbooks inform workplans, what language to use (especially jargon and acronyms), and recommended work cadence, and the nature of the work becomes very predictable. There may not be any room for experimentation or thinking outside the box. With more scale, sometimes that's reasonably expected as teams need to stabilize the boat in choppy waters. New people coming into a company should learn to master the fundamentals of the core business before attempting to change it. I can't fault the desire for predictability in that instance. However, when it comes to innovation, using conventional approaches may actually backfire. As multidisciplinary teams come together, what happens when the playbooks need to blend or intertwine to balance out different working styles? What does it mean to figure out something new versus working on what was previously routine? How will we handle the gaps of understanding between disciplines as they begin to work toward "what's next"? Design is probably the least understood and most underrated entity when the team comes together. Conversely, the designer, product manager, or technologist might struggle to understand what motivates the businessperson. When navigating the pursuit of innovation, we need to overcome these gaps of understanding.

In parallel, as we imagine increasing the representative diversity in our teams, each person brings uniquely different lived experiences. Are we ready to have our playbooks and precedents interrogated by different folks that show up with uniquely different points of view? Are we making them feel welcome to do so? What if they recommend different ways to engage target demographics because they actually come from those demographics and can better appreciate the cultural nuances at play? I've had experience building teams in situations where the present playbooks of the day were not relevant against the new opportunities we faced. We literally had to scour the earth for diverse people who could challenge us with their different perspectives and make us and our methods stronger in relationship to imminent opportunities. After a few years of doing that, I looked back and realized that we had assembled the most diverse team I had ever served and led. Our approach to the work ended up becoming more nimble, fluid, and adaptive to different audiences and needs. With a vibrant mix of races, genders, cultures, backgrounds, and philosophies represented, the teams actually found incredible inspiration from each other. Their aperture was wide open, and they were more astute when nuances emerged in the marketplace. As a result, our methods didn't stagnate to the point of becoming formulaic. Upon reflection, design, with its inherent strength of empathy, served as an important catalyst and leading voice in accelerating these dynamics across our diverse team.

*Nonlinear: Navigating Design with Curiosity and Conviction* illuminates design's nuances and complexities as a source of nonlinear advantage within your multidisciplinary innovation endeavors. Yes, there's actually an advantage to taking a nonlinear, less than formulaic approach! Every step we take in the journey is what I would characterize as a vector. Let's unpack the *Merriam-Webster Dictionary* definition of the word *vector*: "A quantity that has magnitude and direction and that is commonly represented by a directed line segment whose length represents the magnitude and whose orientation in space represents the direction."[1] We can associate the word *magnitude* with the effort or the amount of work you'll put in to fulfill a step in the journey. Then there's the actual direction of that effort. Is it a push to learn more about a target audience? Is it moving forward to commercialize a new solution? Is it pivoting and changing course based on new learnings? Or is it looping back to retread old ground because you discovered a flawed or radically new assumption? I'll use the word *vector* a lot to describe different steps we might take, and I've learned it's not about a right or wrong vector. It's about momentum. There's something to be said for cultivating the momentum necessary to learn as fast as you can before investing everything you have into an idea. You have to make do with the best information you have, one step at a time. Movement will feel like art and science. Movement will involve the left brain and right brain. Movement is further empowered by DEI to ensure that we have brave teams that celebrate people's differences and thus to ensure our aperture is wide open in terms of how we perceive the evolving world.

One of my favorite speeches is from my creative hero Denzel Washington, the famous Hollywood actor, movie director, and Broadway performer. In his commencement address to the 2011 graduating class at the University of Pennsylvania,[2] he said, "To get something you never had, you have to do something you never did," reiterating a growth affirmation received from his wife. Repeating and rehashing what has been done before might be a surefire way to inhibit innovation. Even with the success of design thinking permeating enterprises over the last few decades, we're still at the beginning stages of the business world fully comprehending design and its capabilities. Design is so much more than whiteboarding, Post-it notes, and rapid design sprints. You can't solve all the world's problems in a hackathon or a one-week sprint. The world is far too complicated, and applying formulaic rinse-and-repeat approaches might yield mediocre outcomes or, even worse, induce harm if we don't thoughtfully consider and respect the complexity we're facing. Also, allow me to be a bit frank: Design will not save the world by itself. It can't do it in a vacuum. When partnering at parity with other disciplines at the problem-solving table, then we'll have something. We'll have a shot to use our collective creativity, diversity, and nonlinear approaches to shake things up and inspire meaningful change that we can realize together.

I write these assertions from direct experience navigating situations in which the path wasn't always clear, or I found myself in places where my brewing convictions didn't match what the job or what others expected of me. I was literally in a forest of ambiguity trying to find a new way. I like to use the metaphor of a forest (see figure 1.1) to explain how I think about navigating ambiguity in pursuit of innovation. My proclivity for ambiguity actually started from the very beginning of my career and continues up until this day. Before I go further, I want to be clear that I haven't navigated perfectly. I made plenty of mistakes and hit my head against many brick walls. My hope is that you glean insight from my experiences, both good and bad, to appreciate the nuances of navigating innovation work and understand how your

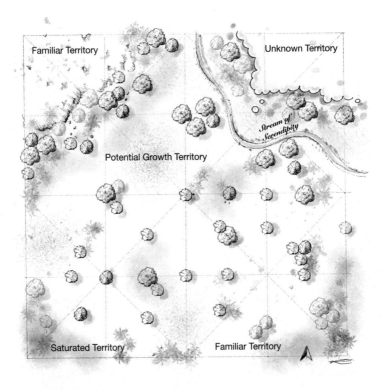

**Figure 1.1**
The metaphorical forest of ambiguity, where we have to navigate different territories with curiosity and conviction to explore what we can learn, what we can find, and what we can create.

career and lived experiences play an important part. No matter the discipline you represent (e.g., businessperson, designer, product manager, or technologist), I will confidently assume that you are a creatively curious person that knows they are navigating a world that's becoming more complex, connected, and accelerated. You need to maneuver in such a way that you can seize that momentum for learning, but perhaps in different ways that you haven't been accustomed to. Because I have had to navigate some early and very unique situations that are now interpreted as multidisciplinary innovation, please allow me to be your guide. Why me? To answer, I'll tell you more about my story of multidisciplinary leaps and lived experiences.

During my youth, when I had glimmers of imagining what I would do for a living, I wrestled with a lot of curiosities. Before work became work, I had hobbies. Mine was drawing. That was my way of seeing the world, interpreting what I saw, and expressing what I conjured up within my imagination. My parents did what they could to feed that creative itch by exposing us kids to a wide variety of things. Being raised predominantly near Detroit, the heart of the American automotive industry, the working culture of the region favored pragmatic disciplines like engineering and business over the arts. Notions of design or innovation were far outside my purview, for right, wrong, or indifferent. I chose mechanical engineering as a first step because of my affinity for math and science, on top of my knack for drawing. I attended the University of Notre Dame and braved the cold weather months navigating its tough engineering curriculum. It was difficult, but the program made me resilient. I learned how to wrestle with problems longer. My engineering education taught me how to make sense of a physical world, to understand how things work. Upon graduation, I channeled my learnings toward one industry that offered a significant runway of opportunity compared to most others. The nuclear power industry hadn't hired young talent for the ten to fifteen years prior to me coming out of school. They were concerned about the drain of knowledge with impending retirements and made an aggressive play for new talent. It was my opportunity to slip through a wide-open door (getting hired by Westinghouse Electric Company) that would lead me to incredible learning opportunities.

As a mechanical engineer, visiting a nuclear power plant in the throes of a maintenance outage was absolutely awe inspiring. When you set foot inside a nuclear containment building, your first instinct is to look up. The sheer size of everything takes your breath away. Steam generators reach up to the upper echelons of the dome-shaped containment building. Looking below your feet (usually through a grated metal floor), you'll peer through several stories of infrastructure, where coolant pumps, piping, instrumentation, and the like all reside deep below. Looking forward, you're greeted with the sight of a very large swimming pool filled with shimmering coolant water of an aqua-blue hue. This water is actually used in the closed operating system when the plant is buttoned up and running at power. As a young engineer, I had to see projects through the steps of discovery, design, engineering, and analysis of hardware solutions; tooling and fabrication; and bringing a complete service intervention to the field to fix or upgrade each plant. I learned a ton through the first few projects, mastered the next few, and eventually had the privilege of leading several end-to-end efforts. Some projects were routine, some projects required new innovative approaches, and some were emergent projects responding to a critical emergency. My technical skills were tested, and my leadership muscles were challenged at every step. In the process, I started to grow curious about the larger strategies surrounding every engineering project and started asking questions in an attempt to comprehend the larger business dynamics at play.

At the same time, I noticed that if you're pretty good at your engineering projects, a company tends to ask you to do that work over and over again, especially as your work directly drives the company's revenues. That's great for folks that love doing that specific work, and there is surely incredible honor in doing it. For me, I felt like a different choice was brewing that would affect the trajectory of my career. I felt I could either double down on my engineering pedigree and become a deeper expert on my projects, or I could widen my aperture to understand those business dynamics that orbited my engineering work. This lingering curiosity drew me to make friends with the marketing department. I found opportunities to engage in stretch assignments in which I could use my engineering experience to help the marketing team inform new proposals. In doing so, I was able to scratch that itch to learn more about commercial matters as we negotiated work with our nuclear-owning utility customers. Despite having my contributions valued, I felt that my business acumen was sorely lacking to be able to connect the dots effectively and command any strategic influence. If I didn't address that gap, my imminent career choice would be made for me, and I knew at the time that I wanted a bit more agency to make that decision for myself.

Fast forward, my curiosities from early commercial exposure led me to pursue an MBA to shore up the language for business I lacked as a technology professional. I attended the Tepper School of Business at Carnegie Mellon University. Tepper was particularly empathetic toward engineers looking to add that layer of business acumen, so it was a great fit for me. I really enjoyed my classes, the faculty, and the Tepper community at large. Their culture embraced this idea of connecting the dots across disparate market forces, and they were willing to change or experiment with their curriculum to match the emerging needs of the marketplace. For example, my MBA journey started in the aftermath of Enron, so ethics became an important thread through several of my classes. Personally, I had to contend with a plethora of new voices and perspectives about what this business degree could mean for me and my future: "To build wealth, you should go into investment banking." "For power and influence, head into management consulting." I felt my own voice withering a bit as I was learning new skills while also trying to envision the type of future that would be right for me. But I did eventually remember that voice of my inner child who used to draw all the time for enjoyment. I let that creative itch begin to guide which companies and industries I pursued. Technology and business models wouldn't be enough; I wanted to join an organization that had creative faculties as well. I wasn't sure what that would mean for me, but I felt my heartstrings being tugged in that direction and looked for companies that embodied a mix of multidisciplinary capabilities.

Companies like Apple and Nike rose to the top of my wish list because they embodied that mix of creativity, business, and technology. I felt I could learn a ton in their environments. I never got a chance to talk with Apple but happened across Nike at an MBA career fair. Thankfully, Nike afforded me a path to join upon graduation. I started as a business planner (a typical post-MBA job) at Nike World Headquarters in Beaverton, Oregon. Our team's mission was to roll up financial and operational performance across different Nike business segments and provide objective analyses to Nike senior executives to help them in their decision-making and quarterly communications with Wall Street. We literally combed through the numbers, unearthed the stories behind the numbers, and wrote the talking scripts that executives would leverage in their conversations with Wall Street analysts during the quarterly earnings release calls: "Why were inventories up? Why was marketing spending down this quarter? Why did gross margins increase?" I was mindful to the needs of this first position, and it surely helped me solidify my business acumen in wrestling with the realities of a publicly traded company of the stature of Nike, Inc. I really appreciated the managers of that group taking a bet on me, someone who didn't come from a conventional business background from the very start of my career.

However, I was truly a product person at heart. I didn't want my business experiences to take me completely away from product, nor the art of invention. To scratch my product itch, I started networking across Nike to look for those kindred spirits doing that type of work. One coffee chat led to another, and so on, until I found opportunities to engage in stretch assignments (i.e., side hustles) to learn from those teams while also showcasing my potential through the act of doing. Eventually, I was able to navigate over to Nike's global footwear product engine, where I encountered professional design being practiced for the first time in my career. Design was also nested in close collaboration with engineering, product management, and business. I knew it was the right environment for me to ask a lot of questions and observe their methods. While making friends among the design community, I shared drawings that reflected my hobby and raw creative skill. Conversations with superstar creatives such as Tinker Hatfield, Angela Snow, Michael DiTullo, Albert Shum, Suzette Henry, Jason Mayden, Jeff Henderson, Natalie Candrian Bell, Eric Avar, and Bruce Kilgore motivated me to keep moving forward in scratching my curiosities. One conversation opened a doorway that would change my life and trajectory. I had a chat with the Jordan footwear design director at the time, a man by the name of D'Wayne Edwards (who is now the president of Pensole Lewis College of Business and Design). He saw my raw creative skill and gave me my first shot to design footwear.

I would meet Edwards in the early mornings to commiserate on a brief that didn't have a designer assigned. After our morning sessions, we would then peel away to do our day jobs, and I would later work on his stuff until the wee hours at night. Rinse and repeat every day for a year, and we birthed two footwear models under my design credits and his mentorship (see figure 1.2). (If you're reading this, D'Wayne, thank you!) That opportunity led to other stretch assignments in different parts of Nike as I continued to cut my teeth on early footwear design work. Little did I know these stretch assignments were bringing me to a major fork in the road. On one hand, I could claw and scratch through more side

**Figure 1.2**
Nike Air Jordan Fusion 8 mid-top and high-top sneakers designed by
Kevin Bethune, under the mentorship of Dr. D'Wayne Edwards and
the Jordan brand at Nike, Inc.

hustles for another ten to fifteen years before I would be fully pedigreed as a footwear designer in Nike's eyes. On the other hand, I could invest deeply into my creative foundation through a different path. By paying attention to how the world was moving outside Nike to appreciate multidisciplinary convergence, I was open to alternative ways to learn and garner more experience. After some soul searching, I chose the alternative path and decided to quit my Nike job to go back to graduate school (I thought I was done with school!) to accelerate my learning. This move would also cement my career positioning to focus on innovation moving forward. To step away from the workforce for another two years meant an incredible sacrifice, but not just for me. My wife was also at Nike, and we just had our first and only son. The evidence trails from my stretch assignments helped her see and believe in my vision. For our son, we eventually wanted this decision to serve as an example of what it means to go after your dreams.

I spent the next two years (or six consecutive semesters) completing a master of science degree in industrial design at ArtCenter College of Design in Pasadena, California. Fast forward: since leaving design school, I've had the privilege of serving as a creative cofounder and executive servant leader in shaping design and innovation capabilities for some really great brands, a couple of innovation platforms, and some really compelling start-ups. A large platform I was able to help shape with material impact was BCG Digital Ventures (BCGDV), a wholly owned subsidiary of the Boston Consulting Group (BCG). Our charter was to work with BCG's clients, navigate an innovation journey with them, and find opportunities to build real businesses to meet real unmet needs.

I came in as an early creative cofounder and left several years later having served as vice president of strategic design for North America, empowering a cohort of over thirty strategic designers, and having global influence for an equal number of designers located in our other international locations. BCGDV has since been folded together with other specialized departments and is now part of BCG.X[3] following an organizational rebranding that occurred after I left. After spending seven years with the founding team, my curiosities drew me to decide to set up my own design and innovation practice in *dreams • design + life*. My company goes after opportunities that address (1) human-centric needs that truly help people unlock their potential or foster human connection beyond pushing digital for digital's sake; and (2) holistic solutions that span physical, digital, or even service-based affordances. Coming up with empathic, intuitive, and holistic solutions was the goal at the company's genesis in 2018.

When I look back to the start of dreams • design + life, I was nervously beginning life as a new entrepreneur without any backing. Just before taking the leap, I had some side-hustle experiments in flight with local start-up friends ahead of my departure from BCGDV and had many colleagues in my primary network signaling that they would be my first clients. At least there was a little evidence in hand to fuel my courage. Going from serving such a busy job and large team at BCGDV to sitting alone in my home studio, the quiet was deafening. Those early weeks were met with an empty inbox, no phone calls, and me keeping myself busy building a sales deck of key offerings that I could articulate to potential clients. I had conceived of a sprint for this type of project, and a sprint for that type of project. I had prices for each, work plans, and legal documents ready to go to execute my first contracts. Although my primary network meant well, I didn't hear from anyone on the other side of my leap. I couldn't fault them; people are busy. If they had a scope of work ready to give me, they surely would. However, some weeks later, the phone started ringing. Folks in my primary network eventually ran across folks in their own networks and were able to play matchmaker. A few months later, I had developed a small roster of clients and a robust pipeline of interesting leads cultivated purely from referrals.

Each inquiry may have started out with a preconceived notion of the work in need (an industrial design, an ethnographic research sprint, a future visioning exercise, etc.) and was probably aligned with how I imagined selling different scopes of work. However, getting into the early rounds of problem-solving, I saw many opportunities to do more than the initial ask. I could lean in and listen to the realities facing my client partners. I could expose them to what I might have been privy to at the time, which is sometimes hard to predict before you actually begin the work. I might have the potential to speak to the competitive landscape, interrogate first principles and core assumptions, or shine a light on different trends to help open their aperture. I learned that I could connect the dots for them in different ways thanks to my multidisciplinary background and unique lived experiences. That became the true nature of my early engagements: less sprint, and more intentional, adaptive, and thoughtful problem-solving. Unlike an agency that may need to apply a sizable project team and bill the client for a full forty hours per week for each person,

I could decide how best to apply my bandwidth and billings in a more fluid manner. On a week-to-week basis, my problem-solving for a given client partner might only occur for a couple days out of that week. I chose to only bill them for that time, usually under an assumed retainer over multiple months of contract. I could spend the balance of my week with other client partners and rinse and repeat each week from there.

This helped my business stay in relationships longer with clients without diminishing our value, while being kind to client budgets in the process. The tact of flexible problem-solving and tolerable billing helped us deliver what clients needed when and where it was necessary in addition to the ability to shift to different priorities over time. In this way, our problem-solving relationship could last over the course of years versus a handful of weeks. When the COVID-19 pandemic drew us into isolation, we tried our best to adapt to the situation through Zoom calls and Slack and Miro digital canvases to accomplish the same approach. During that challenging period, the trust and intimacy of relationships with our client liaisons actually increased. We noticed that their needs extended beyond the design and innovation work into other areas of their business too. I credit the building of trust for enabling the door to widen as much as it did. Aside from designing, I was helping to answer questions such as these: "Is my leadership composition correct?" "Does my team have the right skills for this task?" "How can we attract and retain diverse talent for newly emerging realities?" "Can you join us in presenting our strategies and progress to our board of directors?" Fast forward to today, and my business continues to operate in this very fluid manner. Some weeks, I'm deeply applying my depth of craft on an industrial design problem with my pencil in hand. Another week, I might do some problem-solving over the whiteboard with a team of cofounders. The last seven years have represented a very nonlinear approach to running dreams • design + life, and I'm so grateful.

This has been my polymath journey that I never could have anticipated. When I look back (hindsight being twenty-twenty), I can honestly say that curiosity has been the defining thread through every chapter of experience. Curiosity gave me the itch to experiment. Each experiment bred evidence that gave me courage. A string of evidence over time helped me develop convictions to keep going. I wanted to have a hand in shaping a multidisciplinary future. For someone just hearing about my story, it might seem that things easily snapped into place with every chapter, but that couldn't be further from the truth. First, it wasn't easy approaching the job market as a hybrid with engineering, business, and relatively new design experience. Most companies are wired to celebrate singular disciplines. They didn't know how to place me. Even as an employee with pure intentions to collaborate, I wasn't always welcome to reach out to folks in the next department across from mine because of politics. But the world is changing fast, and its complexity warrants connecting the dots across disciplines more than ever. Second, I am a Black man who has navigated very unique multidisciplinary leaps. I experienced a lot of resistance from those who couldn't see me playing in certain arenas. Constructive critique I will take, but if folks are resisting and not being fully clear about *why*, that forces someone to guess the motivations at play. Is it bias, racism, fear, or ignorance? It's not a great place to be, and that puts a terrible tax on a lot of people vulnerable to marginalization.

Through those experiences, I had to learn that my career was ultimately mine, even amid times of uncertainty. I had to learn that no matter the brand I worked for, and no matter the resistance I faced, I could peer into the world and easily see all kinds of problems and opportunities, waiting for someone to solve them. The landscape is full of gaps, mismatches, cognitive disconnects, latent unmet needs, and numerous forms of exclusion. Unfortunately, very few players are solving them . . . still. I had to look myself in the mirror, and say, "Why not me?" If not me, then who? It's the same for you. If not you, then who? We need to figure out how to align our time, talents, and mindshare against solving the complex needs waiting for us over the horizon. "To get something you never had, you have to do something you never did." This is true no matter your discipline, especially if you want a hand in creating meaningful innovation. You don't have to come from design to be creative; you just have to be creatively curious. If you're from a business, product, or technical background, creativity will prove itself essential within your approach. If you're from design, this book will help you garner more confidence in increasingly complex situations where leveraging design's nuances will be critical for the choices you and your team will make.

As multidisciplinary teams come together in pursuit of innovation, they need to learn how to marry their expertise across the overarching disciplines of business, design, and technology. You could imagine a Venn diagram that illustrates the overlap between these domains. There's magic in the intersections for sure as we explore how the team can work together to surface latent needs and imagine solutions that matter to our audiences (i.e., desirability), show how we can create value (i.e., business viability), and demonstrate that we can make them work (i.e., technical feasibility). But I would argue this is not enough. Our collaboration together should also wrestle with the broader implications of every design, technology, and/or business decision that cascades beyond the team's immediate purview. Collaboration among disciplines should make room to discuss porous topics such as ethics, data privacy, sustainability, and social impact, just to name a few. Even that's not enough. We also need to consider the threads of societal imbalance that have permeated our collective history from way back when and up until our present moment. This multidisciplinary collaboration, along with ample consideration of implications and historical relevance (see figure 1.3), allows the team to begin to see the future more coherently through a number of different vantage points.

If we have that team peer through the looking glass toward the distant time horizon (see figure 1.4), the team members can surface a diversity of data points, inspirations, trends, exemplars, industry paradigms, and human-centric insights. In doing so, they become primed to make natural sparks and connections across richly diverse sets of information. That's setting the stage for creativity. Creativity involves combining existing inputs together in new and novel ways to tell a new story of opportunity. The key word here is *new*. That notion gives me incredible hope that we can conceive better answers than what we have today, and

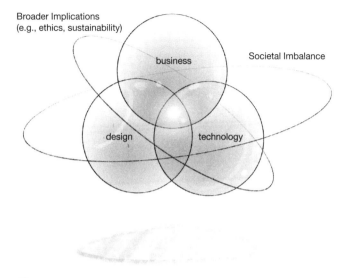

Broader Implications
(e.g., ethics, sustainability)

business

Societal Imbalance

design

technology

**Figure 1.3**
Multidisciplinary teaming across design, business, and technology, while considering broader implications from key decisions and the historical threads of societal imbalance.

hopefully more equitable and respectful ones than what we've experienced in the past. Despite the world being seemingly on fire at any given moment, we might find ways to creatively conjure up new opportunities that crack open the door for change. Creativity definitely implies a serendipity in how these ingredients come together. One might argue that it's hard to manage or difficult to channel. What I can say is that overly formulaic, linear approaches and a lack of multidisciplinary, diverse inputs will cause creativity to stagnate. How do we influence the opposite

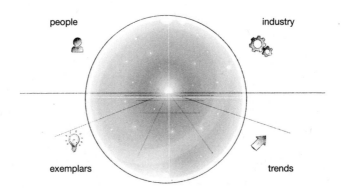

people

industry

exemplars

trends

**Figure 1.4**
Multidisciplinary teaming allows us to see the future via different vantage points as we look through the looking glass toward the distant time horizon.

of that dynamic? What tactics might we use to create more potential for natural serendipity and creative sparks and connections? These questions are what this book wants to explore with you. As you navigate the forest of ambiguity in pursuit of innovation, I hope this book provides some new vectors to help you find your way through what will be a very nonlinear journey.

As we illuminate how *Nonlinear* and its approaches feel in practice, it's important to see yourself playing a role in the journey. This is the case whether you're a designer or coming from a different discipline. As we engage in more multidisciplinary teaming, you will undoubtedly find yourself proximate to certain choices that have the potential to leverage design's nuances and complexities. Therefore, no matter your discipline, you should understand them and foresee how you can influence them, or how your teammates can as well. Bringing your full being, your lived experiences, and your professional expertise to the experience will only make it more meaningful. For example, you may have had exposure to deep quantitative market research if you come from a marketing, business, or data analytics background. *Nonlinear* will show you how that work can actually help frame starting points and boundary conditions for innovation. If you are a software engineer who likes to create prototypes, this book will show you how to contextualize those prototypes to ensure you get the learnings and feedback you need. If you're a designer, this book will show you how to seek the substance to shape your next design iteration and leverage your intuition to make more thoughtful, insightful bets with the time and information you have at your disposal. *Nonlinear* is about breaking linear, formulaic convention and liberating your and your team's creative potential to realize meaningful innovation.

## 2 QUANTITATIVE FRAMING

CREATIVITY NEEDS BOUNDARY CONDITIONS.

While breaking free of formulaic convention in pursuit of innovation, we should also acknowledge that creativity cannot be a free-for-all if we expect to have meaningful impact. In the context of driving innovation and new growth opportunities, we must have some constraints and boundary conditions. I suspect most designers will agree with me in saying that we achieve better design with really good constraints. But how do you get the most out of design in the context of working with a multidisciplinary team? While all disciplines can absolutely exercise and grow their creative muscles, design does need to assert its voice and help the larger team understand its creative potential, while understanding the constraints of the business at the same time. Getting this balance right will surely have a sustaining impact on an enterprise's brand, customer experience, and resonance with customers. For multidisciplinary teams who may not fully comprehend design's potential, an education of design's capabilities may be required. The intention to fill this need may come in two ways. Design will either (1) overtly explain what it does or what it can do for and within the business before actually doing the work, or (2) just demonstrate what it does in the day-to-day work to help drive the business forward. The former runs the risk of being perceived as theoretical or just full of talk. The latter might be more assured because folks may not believe anything until they actually see the work itself.

One of my dear friends and wise mentors is Bob Schwartz, presently Chief Transformation & Innovation Officer at Mount Mary University and former head of design for GE Healthcare. Bob often tells a story about how he tried to win over his executive business stakeholders by explaining how great design was and what it could do for their business. After quickly being yelled out of their office, Bob quickly realized that, instead, he should be more "subversive with a good heart," as he puts it. He figured out a way to use design to advance the business forward and tie design's efforts to the most critical business metrics where all disciplines shared some level of accountability to improve them. Design became an integral and equal part because it could use its knack for creativity, empathy, ideation, and prototyping to help the business move forward and also significantly grow through viable innovation initiatives. He made design work for the multidisciplinary puzzle, and didn't try to force a different, theoretical agenda in isolation. Beating our chests and trying to educate before demonstrating value is usually a lost cause, and unfortunately too many designers hit a brick wall when they try to do this. They wonder why their counterparts start to indirectly reject their voice, perspective, and contributions. We need to interrogate how we can help the business perform, grow, and be better in the end.

However, we should talk about what *better* actually means. Unfortunately, this goes back to our previous conversation on precedents that have influenced business over the course of time. Businesspeople and technologists have had very dominant voices at the problem-solving table, while design is still young to the party. When it comes to perception, the former disciplines get to claim significant credit for the major steps or contributions of any value chain (strategy, research and development, product management, manufacturing, marketing, selling, etc.). Design has been historically perceived as the very last step in the sequence after the others have done all the big thinking and demonstrated their ingenuity. The old adage is that design is there to "put lipstick on a pig" or make the product "look pretty." Perhaps this hasty generalization has lessened thanks to recent efforts to proliferate design thinking and elevate design to the C suite, but when the pen hits the paper, design still has to fight through the perception of just being the last 1 to 5 percent of the value chain in terms of its contribution. I honestly believe that's how the "brief" came to be, no matter if it's given to a design agency or an in-house design team. The big thinking was done already, and the designer needs to execute to the preconceived objectives, scope, and constraints documented within the brief. The expectations have been set.

Let's remember the designer's inherent strength: delivering empathy and compassion in their work with the hope of improving the human condition. Members from other disciplines can absolutely share these qualities too, but designers receive training and specific education that deeply reinforces this approach. By allowing design to participate in all phases of the value chain, from beginning to end, there's a greater likelihood the business will be in better alignment with what people actually want or need. Designers also tend to quickly align to human-centric convictions shared by consumers and broader stakeholders, ranging across sustainability, data ethics, and employee welfare. The more designers are involved, the more that canvases for solving problems can widen and become more porous to include these broader implications that can stem from every design, product, or business decision. A business model that historically indulges in patterns of overconsumption and environmental recklessness might transform into a more respectful business platform that appreciates circular economies, in tune with what customers likely value from the brands they engage. To create this level of impact in alignment with these convictions, designers need to position themselves to empathize with and influence their business and technology teammates, not just the end customer or other stakeholders outside the company's walls.

To better understand the motivations that exist across disciplines in a multidisciplinary team, I've found that language (or fluency) matters a great deal. It really helps you navigate the forest of ambiguity more intuitively with multidisciplinary teams. Folks that encouraged me to pursue an MBA a long time ago likened business concepts to a language that was available for anyone to master, and you didn't necessarily need to pursue an MBA to garner it. Doing things like reading the *Wall Street Journal*, following your favorite stocks, or following an investor segment on the news will do a lot to help you. Of course, an MBA gave me a huge shot in the arm to accelerate my fluency and understanding. I had to figure out how to make that language complement my existing engineering vernacular. Before that, I could speak the language of the critical path, scientific hypotheses, controlled experiments, classical engineering theory, empirical studies, computer simulations, and computer-aided manufacturing, learned from my mechanical engineering education. Design would eventually offer a third layer to my fluency, adding a rich vocabulary covering investigative discovery, empathy, trend curation, future visioning, speculation, creative ideation, prototyping, and soliciting constructive critique. From my early experiences combining these acumens, I've learned how valuable it is to encourage a multidisciplinary team's members to openly discuss their individual motivations and potential areas of conflict sooner than later.

Now, let's drill down into the motivations at play under these languages. The business language often speaks to the need to grow the top line (i.e., revenue) by convincing more customers to engage with a company's offerings, and ideally that company's products and services are more innovative and relevant over time. Every sale requires a cost, or cost of goods sold (COGS), to fulfill it. Ideally, the leftover gross margins are healthy both in terms of absolute dollars and as a percentage of those collected revenues. After expenses associated with business operations and cultivating demand creation (i.e., marketing), we'll have enough earnings left over to invest back into the business and enough free cash flow to keep the business running considering our uses of cash to procure raw materials, manage inventory, and so on. Engineering is motivated to ensure what is being offered for sale actually functions properly and is representative of a high quality in its execution, and that the value chain to make it is reliable, able to produce products with consistency. For innovation specifically, engineering cares about comprehending the degree of complexity and effort required to pull off something new. For design, viable revenue comes from the organization's ability to satiate customer needs and ensure that each offering represents the best form and function to satisfy expectations. In the pursuit of multidisciplinary innovation, we should expect these motivations to hopefully align and work in harmony as much as our languages need to blend together.

Granted, what I just described is a very high-level picture of the key motivations held by each discipline. For any individual that's part of a new multidisciplinary team, really seek to understand your different teammates. In doing so, you'll begin to empathize with what your teammates actually care about and ask better questions of them. At the same time, we must recognize that multidisciplinary convergence is a relatively new phenomenon, and we can't just rest on our laurels and think about our own discipline in a vacuum. Remember that design brief? In the past, it may have been informed by certain points of views that weren't necessarily informed by the designer receiving it, nor was the designer potentially involved in the first place. Same for the engineer. The engineer is often the one fielding the innovation when it has made its way through initial ideation, and they might be catching something downstream that's half-baked. It would be nice to include their views much earlier too. Let's recognize that the newly emerging realities that color our future will require very different behaviors. The designer or engineer doesn't need to necessarily wait for a brief. They can look for signals by proactively leaning in to understand what motivates each discipline around the table, and their ability to ask the right questions will surface new insights to guide the way forward.

To our business colleagues' credit, their motivations tend to root themselves in hard facts and numbers. They leverage quantitative insights from compelling sources of data (financials, market research, etc.) to inform their decisions and strategies over the short and long run. Thanks to the advent of statistics to validate the credence of observed phenomena, they require that the specific insights and data be "statistically significant" to properly be deemed conclusive for making good decisions. Thanks to the sharpening of finance in a world of publicly traded stocks, companies are also hyper aware of how much of any change in a number is considered *material* (i.e., being significant enough to move their earnings per share by a penny). A strategist or finance executive might think twice about approving a business maneuver if it adversely affects that earnings-per-share number by a few pennies (which, multiplied over several million shares, is quite a lot of money). Their job might be on the line over those few pennies. Their incentives may be on the line for those few pennies. Unbeknownst to us, the motivations may cut across disciplines too, and we feel could feel the effects in our bonuses and salary increases in good times, or budget cuts and layoffs in bad times. The numbers represent hard truths in many ways, and we should seek to understand the backstory behind them to inform potential boundary conditions or vectors of potential exploration. The vectors within these stories point to "that's how you can actually make money." They point to "that's how big an audience you might attract."

My last exposure to a heavy concentration of business "numbers" was navigating the global offices of BCG and BCGDV. I've had the privilege of sitting next to *CXOs* (shorthand for any C-level executive, including the chief executive officer [CEO], chief marketing officer [CMO], etc.) across all types of industries and hearing their assessments of how the numbers were rolling in, or how market dynamics were affecting their forecasts and strategies. They needed either BCG's help in partnering to uncover ways to unlock potential value within and adjacent to their operations, or BCGDV's help to innovate, incubate, and commercialize a new-to-the-world business that would yield a material impact on their numbers when combined with their existing platforms. CFOs spoke to their financial results, CMOs interrogated their data analytics and market insights, and CSOs tried to frame their strategic imperatives to balance short- and long-term goals. For design to carve a bit of mindshare in these conversations, I had to learn how to develop my empathy for the framing that mattered to these executives in driving critical business results. Design would need to be a subversive agent to help those business objectives rather than sitting on a soapbox espousing how great design would be for their cause. Otherwise, those folks surely wouldn't listen or take design seriously. Let's cover the key framings important to these leaders and the threads of relatability that design can latch onto to help move the business to a much better place.

## FINANCIAL ANALYSIS

The critical framing for the numbers is how they roll up to inform a company's financial statements. This is the case for both private and publicly traded companies. For those without a finance or accounting background (don't worry!), these statements include (1) a profit and loss statement (P&L), (2) a balance sheet, and (3) a cash flow statement (see figure 2.1).[1] For public companies, anyone can go to the investor page on a company's website and download their 10-Ks (i.e., annual reports) and 10-Qs (i.e., quarterly reports) to understand the financial and operational picture of the company in numbers. For private enterprises, obviously, you would have to be on the inside to see the numbers. Short of being an employee within a private company, you might get some clues from what the private company chooses to share externally through press releases, media affairs, or participating in external market research studies. You should find what you can and try to avoid feeling intimidated when diving into this material. Just like you can tell a story by drawing an illustration with a no. 2 pencil, the numbers also tell a story through dollars and cents. The cool thing is that the structure of how the numbers are presented is relatively the same from company to company, making comparisons between your company and the next company easy to manage in order to glean more stories about your organization's specific performance in comparison to other organizations.

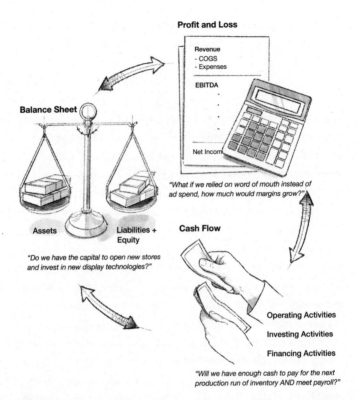

**Figure 2.1**

Financial statements offer a standard framework to investigate the stories behind the numbers and the flow of money within a company.

These statements help business leaders break down and evaluate the financial and operational performance of a company. Every line item across the three statements contains a story in some way. In fact, in my business planning role at Nike, we had to supply written (almost journalistic) commentary on the backstory behind every number or change within each financial report. When providing updates on why certain items were up or down over a given quarter, having the backstory was essential to fuel understanding of the key reasons behind any movements. Aside from ensuring an entity remains a viable operation, external stakeholders need these statements to understand where a company is headed within a dynamic market landscape. Wall Street or a community of investors need to understand an entities recent progress as it relates to revenue growth, free cash flows, and earnings per share. These signals allow them to project forward and forecast the attractiveness of an investment based on anticipated returns and financial upside. Internally, we need to ensure everyone understands the forward-looking story as documented in the business's forecasts. In my Nike planning experience, this ensured our leaders were armed with the soundbites necessary to engage Wall Street effectively on earnings calls and convey a sense of confidence about the company's future.

Wall Street will channel its perceptions into solidifying a point of view on the valuation (i.e., underwritten value) of a public company, translated into the price per share of its common stock. Wall Street rarely rewards a company for what it did in the recent past. Instead, it rewards a company on what it thinks it will do in the near and distant future. It will demote a company's price based on problems (e.g., inventories piling up that could erode gross margins downstream) that it may perceive from their numbers as it relates to their ability to navigate profitably in a dynamic market. What informs that sense of future inside a company? *Strategy.* Strategy represents a series of tactics to put the business on better footing over time. Achieving better footing may translate into more top-line revenues (*top line* referring to the fact that revenue is the first line item at the top of the P&L). Better footing may translate into capturing market share and enjoying increased profitability by making smart moves with company expenses. Enterprise leaders must organize, prioritize, and sequence the tactics that will help realize these results as ultimately reflected in the financial statements and forecasts. Now that we have a sense of this framing of what's necessary to keep a business viable and well perceived in the case of Wall Street, we can shift our attention to strategic framing. What are the tactics that will increase revenues, reduce expenses, and expand profitability in the end? We need to first look to the stakeholders we serve or intend to serve across the market landscape.

At this point, I need to offer an important caveat. Across this book, I will speak to experiences I've had mostly serving for-profit enterprises. However, I believe the principles are still generally applicable if we're talking about different archetypes of entities like nongovernmental organizations (NGOs), governments, or institutions. They all need to collect proceeds, garner cash flow to operate, curb expenses, and ensure they stay on budget, even if expanding profitability may not be their goal. At least we can level-set and agree they want to remain viable organizations no matter the shape of entity. For any enterprise that aims to grow, we need to understand an entity's recent history to understand where it sits in relationship to emerging opportunities. How has the organization been able to perform, financially and operationally speaking? For public companies, we can get some of this perspective by reading their 10Ks and 10Qs. If I'm entering into a business relationship with a company (e.g., soliciting my services to them), I may need to submit a data request, with the hope that I might get a host of financial, operational, strategic planning, and even market research materials to inform our initial understanding of the company's performance before we hypothesize any solution or initial vectors of investigation. Whether this has to be requested or is available publicly, we need to collect any information we can to get to the stories that are waiting to be unlocked from the numbers.

## MARKET RESEARCH AND SIZING

The next questions become: Where did those sales come from to generate the revenues that we observe? Which customers and demographic segments were responsible? What is their breakdown, demographically speaking (age, gender, race, income, education, etc.)? Where are they coming from geographically speaking (city, state, country, rural, urban, language, etc.)? How might we segment them in terms of their spending levels (i.e., discretionary income) and their purchasing behaviors, working down from highly engaged segments (e.g., upper decile or quartile of spending) to the least engaged segments? What clues can we infer about their purchasing behavior and the ways they shop for new offerings? What can we infer about their psychographic tendencies (preferences, values, personal goals, ambitions, personality traits, etc.)? By parsing the data, hopefully will get a sense of the drivers that make up how we're collecting proceeds to fuel our enterprise. We do not have to treat these drivers in isolation. Chances are, there are correlations that might be understood by feeding our data into a computer to create regressive models that show how much one variable might influences other variables, and how those patterns and relationships feed toward the aggregated result we see in the top-line revenue number or the company's ability to capture market share.

Aside from understanding which customers inform revenue, we also need to understand who we don't have as potential customers. That could be equally, if not more, important in some cases and may require additional market research to ascertain how big of a total addressable market (TAM) we're missing. Typically, most enterprises will prioritize activating a market research sprint with either in-house research teams or external agency partners. To understand how big of a population there might be, quantitative research is usually the go-to vehicle in the form of quantitative market surveys that solicit insights from large sample size populations (i.e., a big $n$ sample size) that will yield statistically significant, conclusive insights. Thanks to digital channels, it's relatively easy to seed a survey for a massive population via platforms like Survey Monkey.[2] With the advent of social media platforms, we might consider using digital growth marketing techniques (e.g., seeding spot ads on social media or creating simple landing pages) to run tests and garner more quantitative feedback. We can instrument these digital properties with simple calls to action (CTAs) to allow potential customers to signal how they might self-identify or what they might prefer based on a myriad of options or concepts we put in front of them.

Whether through conventional quantitative surveys or leveraging growth marketing analytics from platforms like Facebook, we can infer how someone self-identifies within a large population. We can infer what they do by the activities and behaviors they self-select or opt into as they fill out our surveys or engage our seeded ad placements online. We might ask them deliberately how they might choose particular options placed in front of them. These could be choices that serve up potential products, platforms, or services that they might consider in isolation with other choices. We could ask for their deliberate choice via a simple multiple-choice question, or present three CTAs on a social media ad and see which one they pick. If we want to get more sophisticated, we could use techniques like MaxDiff (i.e., best-worse) quantitative analysis, where we might float a larger number of potential choices and see how much they prefer one option among a handful of other options and gauge the relative indexing of preferences within the proposed set of choices. Maybe the choices we serve up are indicative of the current-state feature sets that we might already be selling, or we might have a preliminary hypothesis for new feature sets that we could offer but need more data to test their potential relevance. MaxDiff could give us richer fidelity to make the most informed decision.

Through this additional research on potentially new target audiences, we can parse the data the same way as we did for existing customers. We can comprehend how the data breaks out by demographics, geography, and psychographic affinities. This is especially valuable to help us frame the market landscape and decide where we should spend our time exploring innovation and growth opportunities. Let's remember the visual metaphor of a forest of ambiguity from chapter 1 to bring this to life. As we navigate the forest in pursuit of opportunities, we might play the analogous role of a land surveyor. Whether we want to study what is sitting on the land, dig into the earth, or map the topology, we have to use the best instruments we have to figure things out one section of forest at a time. Before we touch a shovel, we should know exactly where we should be digging and for what purpose. Quantitative market research helps us survey the landscape appropriately (see figure 2.2) to understand where its best to place our bets, and potentially with whom to do so. It also helps determine where we shouldn't waste the team's time and resources. We also have to recognize that the act of surveying is just the start to the journey, much like the land surveyor who needs to completely map out the land before they bring in the heavy equipment to start digging.

## STRATEGIC FRAMING

As mentioned before, strategy represents the series of tactics we map out over time to achieve our short- and long-term objectives. By leveraging enough financial understanding of our company's performance and enough awareness of how we're positioned in the market, we have a shot at crafting a coherent strategy to journey forward so long as we have enough conclusive data to guide

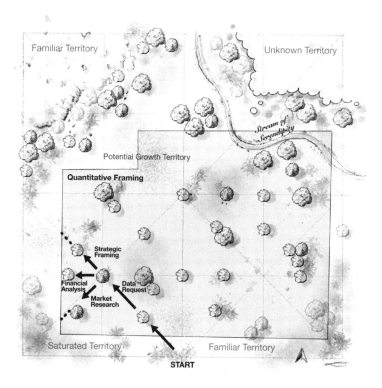

**Figure 2.2**
Surveying the market landscape as we navigate the forest of ambiguity using quantitative data to strategically frame boundary conditions.

our steps, one move at a time. The key word here is *conclusive*. This conclusive data helps us decide when and where to prioritize our team's time and resources. "Do we get higher gross margin with this consumer if we address their needs over here, or should we be talking to another audience over there?" Without that data, we risk precious time and resources if our bets aren't framed in the right places or along the most relevant vectors of exploration. We also have to realize that we are not the only ones taking a journey across the landscape. Our competitors would love to outpace us and capture our market share. There are also substitute offerings that could steal the mindshare of our audiences too. Also, rarely does a company have all the resources to build its own value chain from the ground up themselves. To deliver their offerings, they likely need buyers and suppliers involved to help sustain their operations. All these elements need to be considered when we think about our strategies within the context of the market landscape.

Thanks to popular business frameworks like Porter's five forces, we can inventory all the entities that we may have to contend with or manage within our landscape (see figure 2.3).[3] From a competitive positioning standpoint, our company and competitors that look similar to us are competing for each other's market share. Competitive advantage is also established in how we deal with the potential buyers of our products and services, no matter if the business model is business to business (B2B) or business to consumer (B2C). We need to consider potential buyers' bargaining power in the type of orders and deals they can broker with us. Are we vulnerable to risk in our dealings with potential

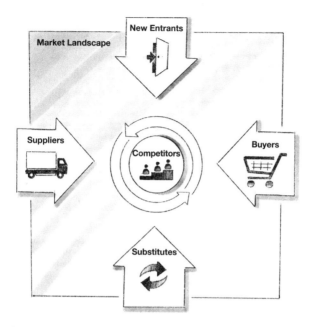

**Figure 2.3**

Porter's five forces is a popular strategic framework to dissect a marketplace and study the moves of the different players within it.

buyers? Could they abandon us at a moment's notice for a better price elsewhere? We need to consider these realities in our tactics. The same is true for the suppliers we deal with to inform our value propositions, products, and services. Do we have bargaining power with our suppliers? If one supplier were to fold, is there an alternative supplier accessible to replace them? We can easily be at an advantage or disadvantage if we're not careful. Finally, let's not forget new entrants that might not look like direct competitors, but have the power to disrupt the space of our investigation. Large tech firms (e.g., Google, Uber) typically fit this category with their platforms that serve millions, if not billions, of people. They can easily divert consumer mindshare away from incumbent players using technology or unique intellectual property.

The idea of all these players navigating the same landscape might feel a bit intimidating. If we manage a company with an existing platform of products and services, we want it to remain relevant and differentiated for the foreseeable future. We want to keep our stakeholders and consumers engaged when they probably have other choices that could attract their attention. On the flip side, the landscape offers a lot of different nutrients if we're thinking about creating new solutions for an emerging opportunity. In a way, we might think about identifying capabilities that already exist in the market, even though they may be represented as competitors, buyers, suppliers, entrants, or substitutes. If we imagine bringing new solutions to market, we should remember that we don't have to build everything ourselves. We might build some pieces, but we could also partner with existing players in the same market. Through mergers and acquisitions, we might acquire a start-up to absorb its capabilities and make them ours. We might collaborate with the competition if it makes sense to scale our efforts together and grow the market together. Some industries call that "coop-etition." Ultimately, we should scan the marketplace through our creative lens to imagine all the different ways we can shape a new value stream to make our innovation successful. For now, we've at least established a strategic framing to evaluate the market landscape and all the players that move within it.

Across financial analysis, market landscaping, and strategic framing, we have the opportunity to use our capabilities to uncover new boundary conditions as we scan the forest of ambiguity. Unlocking the stories behind the numbers will give us an understanding of the key drivers for a company and allow us to decide where to make the best use of our time and limited resources. Within a multidisciplinary team, you can lean into your business teammates to have them explain what they see from the numbers. Understand their point of view (POV), but don't be overly deferential. Whether they are part of your team or not, dive into this material yourself to get a sense of what's happening. You get to decide whether it's something you want to use to inform your starting points for investigation or challenge it as a way to open the aperture. Really listen to your hunches while the data is speaking to you. Despite the business-centric POV you uncover, there might be conversative positions that shroud potentially latent opportunities from your immediate purview. At least let this information be a guide to help you frame where to start, whether it's within the envelope of this rationale or your brewing sense that you should defy convention and explore to the contrary. Remember, these capabilities offer a starting point for us to investigate and explore further. You're never wrong if you keep moving and learning.

· · ·

## Takeaways: Finding Stories in the Numbers

• Lean into developing your fluency for what motivates other disciplines around the problem-solving table. Doing so will help you better empathize with your teammates. The team doesn't need to wait for the brief to understand what drives the business forward toward its goals.

• Leverage the context that financial statements, market research, and strategic framing provide you to understand the boundary conditions and which vectors are worth exploring, which opportunity spaces are worth prioritizing, and how you might strengthen initial hypotheses.

• Avoid being overly deferential to the question, "What does the data say?" Quantitative research and the numbers help us strategically frame where we spend our time, but we still have to dig for substance. We need to find the substance that speaks to attitudes, behaviors, and unmet needs.

## 3  QUALITATIVE DESIGN INVESTIGATION

UNCOVERING THE SUBSTANCE OF LATENT INSIGHTS.

In my professional journey, data to inform our quantitative framing was always plentiful or, at least to a degree, accessible. Sure, it may have taken some additional work to conduct primary market research, instrument growth marketing tactics, or dive into secondary desk research, but at least the data was in arm's reach whenever we needed it. When getting a taste of relevant data, teams will quickly triangulate a hypothesis and move that hypothesis forward as a vector until more data is collected to challenge or refute it. With data impinging on us from every direction, we have the benefit of speed as we comb and collect data from available sources. Advanced connectivity and the speed of digital computation further exacerbate our thirst for it. But are we getting everything we need, and at the right fidelity of understanding? I believe teams typically seek data to either validate a hypothesis or inform the decisions that we need to make substantial progress against a preconceived agenda. Do we prioritize this project over that project, based on available data? Will this initiative generate a stronger financial return than that initiative, based on available data? Do we understand how much this demographic of consumers is willing to pay for a given product, based on observed engagement data?

The data required to inform a decision is usually pretty conclusive in nature. It's the type of data that states a matter of fact: From a finance perspective, revenues grew 15 percent, year over year. Gross margins need to increase by fifty basis points (or +0.5 percent) from 34.5 percent last quarter to 35.0 percent this quarter. From a market research perspective, the last quantitative survey showed our top decile of consumers spent $150 on average each month with us and tend to choose option C over options A and B with statistical significance. This growth marketing test shows that visitors typically bounce from our website after getting 50 percent through the landing page upon scrolling down before going somewhere else. From a strategic framing perspective, we know we're dealing with a *red ocean* (i.e., crowded) market landscape due to the flood of similar competitors (i.e., a data point in its own right) that have entered over the past eighteen months. These facts help us understand potential vectors at our disposal. These data points help us understand numerical trends. These data points, in some ways, may be absolutes. They help us compare. They help us decide. At the same time, the depth of insight from them is actually very shallow. The fact is the fact, and there's not much more we can say about it.

Conclusive, quantified data gives us the confidence to make decisions that have significance to our organizations. Of course, the opposite is true. Without good data, bad decisions could have material consequences on our financial or operational performance. Ideally, we should ensure we always have good data available. Then what? When it's time to engage that actual opportunity, do we have the richer, qualitative substance or depth of insight necessary to shape new ideas and solutions? In my experience, this substance has been typically missing at the very start of most innovation journeys. That's fine to recognize the gap in its own right, but in a world accelerating faster thanks to digital, too many teams are navigating fast without this substance and feeling way too confident in what the quantitative data is telling them. With a desire to move fast and throw stuff up on the wall, sometimes we actually need to slow down and invest more time looking for richer, qualitative substance. It becomes unfortunate when team members speak about the need to talk to their audiences, and that inquiry is suppressed based on the paradigm to "move fast and break things" without any bandwidth to really engage people in a thoughtful way. Without robust qualitative insights, we risk moving forward with ignorance and bias. We also risk producing a lot of follow-on, commodity solutions that are reflective of the lack of substance that would have been needed to truly set ourselves apart.

Now, the idea of seeking qualitative insights can bring its own special baggage. Typically, in my experience, most organizations resort to two conventional techniques to fulfill this need. First, they may run focus groups to solicit consumer attitudes and preferences through qualitative surveying. Usually, the aim is to test or validate a given set of hypotheses or assumptions. You can imagine a handful of folks in a conference room being questioned for their thoughts or shown visuals of features to gage preferences. Second, enterprise teams may arrange in-depth, one-on-one interviews with individuals that best represent their target audiences. Despite this precedent, we should take a step back and realize how much the market research landscape has changed over the last few decades. While I was studying at ArtCenter, a professor by the name of Katherine Bennett really opened my eyes to the power of qualitative research through the lens of design investigation. Bennett offered a wealth of experience working close to design luminaries like Henry Dreyfuss and Stephen Hauser—not easy as a women trailblazer in her field. Bennett and I had a chance to catch up over Zoom during the writing of this book, and I'll include a few reinforcements from her (and my way of honoring her influence on me).[1] Bennett exposed me to many thought leaders in the design research landscape, from renowned experts John Zeisel to Elizabeth B.-N. Sanders.[2] Figure 3.1 takes inspiration from Sanders's work, which characterizes the research landscape along a few dimensions to help us understand the myriad of qualitative research techniques available.

On the left-hand side, we have the expert-driven mindset where folks we engage are seen as subjects through the lens of our expertise (marketing, sales, product, etc.). You can imagine experts in white coats carrying clipboards and studying their subjects in a focus group environment from behind a mirrored glass. There's an implied hierarchy with that image: expert and subject. On the

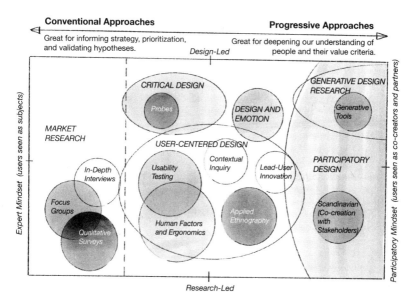

**Figure 3.1**

Qualitative research landscape adapted from the work of renowned design research expert Elizabeth B.-N. Sanders, PhD, at Ohio State University.

right side, we have progressive, participatory mindsets where we aim to co-create with our stakeholders in a workshop or out in the field in their context, treating them as equals. From the bottom, we might approach from a research-led curiosity, leveraging investigation approaches that are structured, regimented, and almost scientific in their nature. We might see this manifest in the form of focus groups, ergonomic studies, and applied ethnography through one-on-one interviews. From the top, we may be more design-led and actually make something, just to get people to react to a stimulus and share what they think about it. This represents a unique opportunity for design to use its gifts of visualization, storytelling, and prototyping. This can come in the form of designing probes or speculative prototypes to stimulate conversation. For participatory formats, we can leverage design to make generative tools to foster idea generation within small groups. I've seen this take the form of having groups build Lego models in response to a question or putting predesigned components of a story in front of people and allowing them to structure their own story using generative inputs.

Across the landscape in figure 3.1, there are many detailed methodologies that practitioners have codified to serve different purposes. There are numerous books you can find on each approach. When I studied at ArtCenter, we were encouraged to use our judgment to make the best choices among the different methods available. We had to imagine what we hoped to learn from the audiences we engaged. Would we want to hear what people had to say about a particular topic? Would we want to observe what they do? Would we want to probe for deeper beliefs? There were so many research intents to consider. Before ArtCenter, I remember feeling the bias inherent in the conventional approaches I witnessed within companies. Most teams generally had an idea of what they wanted to achieve anyway, and they were seeking only to validate their thinking, even if their expressed intent was to learn what motivated their audiences. The research takeaways tended to amplify those insights that echoed team consensus. But if we try different approaches around the research landscape, we can develop a plurality to the perspectives and conclusions that are gleaned from multiple vantage points. Consensus might be challenged in a good way. We can gain understanding of what people are saying, believing, thinking, feeling, and emoting. We stand a chance of understanding who these people are at a deeper level. We might learn how they self-identify, their underlying cognition, and the lenses through which they interpret and navigate their world.

## INVESTIGATING STAKEHOLDER NEEDS IN BIOTECH

A recent example of navigating qualitative investigation occurred with a long-time client and biotech startup called Invoy, based in Irvine, California.[3] Invoy is led by founder and CEO Lubna Ahmad, PhD, and its value proposition is aimed directly at the weight-management space. With Invoy, a member wakes up and exhales into a breath device every morning. Using the Invoy app, they reflect on their behaviors (e.g., diet, exercise, habits, events, and any negative symptoms) over the past twenty-four hours while the breath analysis is running. The member is connected to an Invoy program analyst, who helps connect the dots between the breath data and the reflected behaviors to provide specific recommendations, from goal setting to meal planning. I was introduced to Ahmad through a former colleague just as I was starting dreams • design + life. Invoy's genesis came from Ahmad's doctoral research in respiratory chemistry, and was further incubated to address children's obesity, then health for low socioeconomic families, and then enterprise employers who were eager to provide Invoy to their employees to give them better weight-management tools. Ahmad's passion for healthcare came from health challenges during her youth, and her dedication to healthcare has been steadfast ever since. Advancing her research as a scientist attracted benefactors who convinced her she could raise money and start a company: scientist turned CEO. I made the drive down to Irvine to meet her under the premise that I might be able to help with some industrial design needs.

When we sat down, we just started talking. Talking led to whiteboarding, and we sketched out Invoy's existing customers, potentially new audiences they could attract, their value chain, and their unique intellectual property. This whiteboarding led to natural questions and the surfacing of new vectors of opportunity that we could consider exploring in our newfound working relationship. This first meeting led to a few more meetings, and we eventually established a weekly routine of problem-solving. What really struck me was Ahmad's open mindedness toward problem-solving with someone (me) who could offer a very different perspective. On top of that, she was very open to what design could bring to her platform. She would eventually invite design's contributions into every facet of her company. We formed a professional relationship based on trust, based on the regular creation of tangible evidence that really moved the business. I realized that Invoy offered another rare, future-forward runway where we could demonstrate design's potential at parity with engineering, science, and business. Ahmad's trust allowed me to find permanent design talent for Invoy as well, resulting in multiple hires. In our last one-on-one over a Zoom call, Ahmad offered some thoughtful reflections of our early journey working together:

I viewed you [Bethune] as a man of character, technically proficient and extremely good at drawing, and you valued and appreciated the business reality and the business context . . . but had a maniacal pursuit of making sure the short term was heading in a direction of the long term.

I do think that one thing that's very unique about your background . . . the fact that you've been classically trained in very different disciplines . . . opens up the way you view things to a more holistic . . . and perhaps in that sense a more complete point of view, that actually aggregates different places that people would perceive to be very disconnected. The way you view design, it transcends the idiosyncrasies of any one part of an organization, or any one discipline, in maniacal pursuit of what is the true solution to a significant problem.

I thought it was really quite remarkable that you were able to take a pretty significant data dump of what I thought was seemingly random and disconnected facts that were relevant to solving a complex problem, and recognizing themes that served as guideposts.

Through our journey, I asked myself: What is the purpose behind design? Is it engineering? Is it product? . . . What is it? It wasn't really research either. It was this other area that served as a distillation of a North Star and a mandate that crossed (to a certain extent) all disciplines to move nonlinearly towards a North Star. I think that piece was probably the most meaningful impression of you.

When we think about different guide rails, I think there was an element of design across our disciplines. I think the reason was to make sure everyone was marching toward a North Star. I think it was interesting, in defining that North Star, how uncompromising you were to the balance between *quant* and *qual*, when it came to what the product and the company had to do and its mission.

Having that five- to ten-year-out view is "impossible" and also required for early-stage ventures that are trying to solve a really big problem. Absent there being a function within the organization that is making that important to talk about today, I think it's very easy to lose the soul of the company.[4]

In the process of this budding relationship, what really made me latch onto Invoy's mission was following Ahmad on a multicity "listening tour," where we searched for latent insights from a mix of different stakeholders to guide our roadmap of priorities. Across stops in Miami, New York, Charlotte, and Southern California, we talked with existing Invoy members about their experience, local clinicians interested in Invoy for their patients, and executive stakeholders that could potentially introduce Invoy to willing customers within their organizations. As a new-to-the-world venture, I expected a CEO to always wear her commercial "hat" to sell the company in those stakeholder conversations. However, this was not the case. First, I felt a deep sense of appreciation for Ahmad from the existing members who've been using the service over an extensive period of time, sometimes more than twelve to eighteen months in some cases. Second, she was literally snapping into the mode of a "coach" in her interactions with the people we engaged, no matter if it was meeting an active Invoy member at a Starbucks or stepping into the C-suite to talk with a team of executives. Ahmad consistently delivered her objective expertise with a compassionate, human touch. She truly wants to help everyone she encounters with authentic convictions.

To prepare for this listening tour, we deliberately took some time to think about different vectors of qualitative investigation based on the nature of our curiosities. Figure 3.2 brings this to life in a simple visual, inspired by a more comprehensive "tool picker" framework created by Katherine Bennett to guide her students in crafting the most fitting design investigative strategy.[5] If we wanted to understand what people do and the specific journey

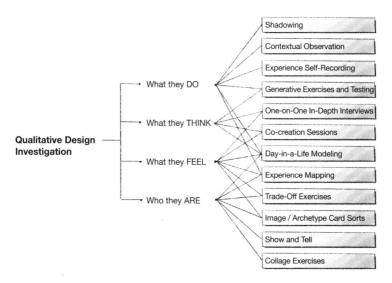

**Figure 3.2**

A qualitative research decision tree inspired by and adapted from Art-
Center Professor Katherine Bennett's tool picker framework.

they take without us intruding or coloring what they might do, we
might shadow them or observe them from a distance. If we want
to understand their motivations, we might get them to choose
a few items from among a pile of visuals and explain why. We
might get them to make trade-offs between a finite set of generative materials. If we want to understand who they are, we might
ask them to select from a set of descriptors, archetypes, or visual
analogies and explain the rationale behind their choices (see figure 3.3). Among these potential vectors of investigation, we might
have risked a bit of "analysis paralysis" to decide the best tactics.

"When I use that product, I tend to feel more like the ruler ... an authority"

**Figure 3.3**
Generative tools may include exercises such as archetype card sorts, in which participants are expected to make choices and articulate their reasons why.

However, experience tells me that the best approach is to just get started with humility and see what vectors of investigation feel most appropriate from your initial conversations with people. Did you learn something new? Then next, take the next step that intuitively feels right. This is a nonlinear and nuanced dance, and the Invoy listening tour provided a compelling runway to try some different things.

Upon landing in the first city on the tour, our first job was to get each person to recount their experience with weight management and what it's been like to use Invoy's service. We couldn't just ask them a battery of questions and expect them to reveal their deepest thoughts outright. We had to pull from a number of different techniques to inform a strategy for each individual conversation. Instead of a regimented discussion guide informed with a battery of questions, we created an organic set of stimuli to provoke and foster deeper conversations. We chose not to include interrogations about whether they liked this feature or that feature; instead, we constructed more open-ended questions just to get people talking and sharing their personal stories with weight management and weight loss. We wanted to understand their unmet aspirations as well as their concrete constraints within each topic. If you will bear a tennis analogy for a moment, we wanted to volley the first question and see how the participant would respond to it. Based on their initial response, we would ask more probing questions along the same thread. This approach is sometimes referred to as the *five whys* technique because you have an opportunity to drill into and dissect the initial response to encourage the sharing of even more relevant information that might be hiding behind the initial response.[6]

In some conversations, we put the current-state Invoy products in front of participants and asked them to perform a breath test and talk through the pros and cons of their experience. We closely observed the micro-interactions with every movement as they performed their breath tests, and only subtly nudged with provocations of "Tell me more?," "How come?," and "That's interesting, what else?" Sometimes we would parrot what they just did, to show them a mirror of the interaction and see what further explanation they could offer. In other conversations, we wanted to get to know them and their relationship to weight management in general. We couldn't start out by simply stating, "tell us about your weight loss journey," and expect them to offer any depth. Weight by itself is a very sensitive topic for most people. To get them in a more constructive mindset, we created generative canvases. When it was time to talk about it, we slid a blank canvas in front of them, and asked them to literally draw out their journey of how weight has played a role in their life. Becoming a parent, experiencing loss, or a health challenge may have been some of the triggers for weight gain. We reinforced that there were no right or wrong answers and just asked them to scribble out the best depiction of their journey. Getting their arms and hands moving to draw something while speaking took their minds to a very different place. The visual exercise provided a safe space to go into their feelings and unearth their experiences versus tripping up on the stigma of weight and feeling like a failure. Ahmad offered more reflections of how this felt for her:

> If it were left to me, I would have pursued the conversations in a substantially more structured fashion. You welcomed and embraced a very significant level of openness in the conversations.
>
> During our travels, I remember I was talking about the role of AI and technology in scaling things. You kept on insisting that the human touch is what you were observing, and that we have to scale the human touch. I thought that was an interesting component of messaging that I think is lost in a lot of tech companies. The way a person feels can be scaled, and people can become your ambassadors of change. That's more powerful than the technology alone.

I also thought it was really interesting that you made everyone (all the participants) draw, which feels like the most anti-spreadsheet thing you could do. Especially for something as complex as weight management and your health, the ability to distill that down to a set of childhood images or stuff you don't want to talk about . . . to have the flexibility and space to draw that out on a sheet of paper. That was a particularly powerful way of helping somebody connect with parts of their own existence that they might not directly relate to. That wiring of right brain—left brain is really important for people to see connections that they otherwise perhaps would not have seen.[7]

We exercised similar generative approaches when testing respondents' reactions to our early thinking for future solutions. For stimulus, we created more canvases with low-fidelity, sketchy images of potential product directions and use cases. We were quick to explain that we wanted to share rough, early ideas, and solicit respondents' feedback to make them better. The low-fidelity sketches (see figure 3.4) were almost cartoon-like to purposely convey that they were unfinished ideas. We wanted respondents' frank and honest feedback and, even better, their own ideas on how to improve our thinking. If the sketches and illustrations were too tightly designed, then someone might be too nervous to give authentic feedback for fear of offending us. Instead, our visuals opened the conversation up. We encouraged the participant to feel empowered to co-create better answers alongside us. I sometimes demonstrated this by simply scribbling right on top of one of the sketches to show participants that we can safely cross out a sketch and start over. We recorded their reactions, but also solicited their input and even put the pencil in their hands to allow them to draw too. Authentic co-creation was our ambition, and we surely witnessed it as our conversation tables were filled

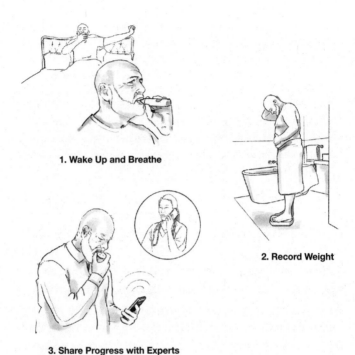

1. Wake Up and Breathe

2. Record Weight

3. Share Progress with Experts

**Figure 3.4**
Low-fidelity sketches and storyboards serve as helpful visual stimuli for ethnographic conversations with key stakeholders.

with plenty of doodles all over our stimuli. Even when socializing new ideas, when people feel empowered to make things together (and make existing ideas better), we always come out better on the other side of the conversation.

When it comes to qualitative investigation, I remember those projects in my career when there was just no time, and folks were itching to get their interviews done and hand over the takeaways to the next team. I look back and imagine the formulaic tendencies, the biases and ignorance that going fast bred by default. I remember watching how subject matter experts might engage these participants too. They sometimes mischaracterized participants as merely ignorant subjects to study, filling out worksheets on their clipboards as a person talked. I try not to judge someone pressed for time and juggling many urgent priorities, but this type of fast-twitch qualitative research behavior is surely harmful. This harm will cascade in the shape of ill-informed assumptions that make their way into future products and services at scale. A deeper dose of humility is sorely needed no matter the research approach. I believe one must have a mindset to engage participants at the most humane level possible with compassion and empathy. I would rather meet someone who's comfortable having a conversation at Starbucks than talk to them in a sterile focus group environment. I would rather tout myself as a design professional just trying to make the right thing and not claiming to know everything about a topic. They probably have a lot more substance to teach me and my teams from their lived experience. I view participants who are gracious enough to share their time and ideas with the utmost gratitude. I need them to succeed.

## DISTILLING LEARNINGS INTO SYNTHESIS

Thankfully, the partnership with Invoy afforded us a runway to engage people authentically around their most sensitive challenges with weight. At the same time, we weren't immune to the pressure to translate our findings into actionable insights and opportunities. We couldn't hand the stack of meeting transcripts and scribbled-up canvases to the next team and say, "here you go." We had to put in a lot of work to distill the key latent insights that would compel us to start generating ideas. We needed to establish new anchors in the forest of ambiguity, to give us solid footing to define the next set of moves that we could make. Among the reams of notepaper, video interview footage, and audio iPhone recordings, we had to take some time and fully immerse ourselves in these materials. We had to take the time to be sure we weren't glossing over important substance. We needed to feel confident that we'd uncovered the less-than-obvious stuff that sits beyond the present consensus of what our teams know already. We literally carved out several days to relisten to recordings and jot down time-stamped notes on the interesting things we heard or observed. In my design training, this activity was called *codification*. Aside from verbatims, we paid close attention to video footage of someone's body language shifting. We jotted notes to ourselves of the observation if it was a clue that we might triangulate with other observations.

For those of us who were directly involved in the interviews or reviewed the video transcripts, we took our respective piles of Post-it notes from the codification work and walked them into an

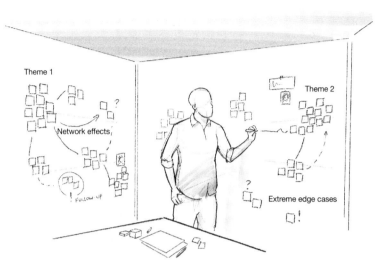

**Figure 3.5**
Affinity mapping exercise in which designers use abductive thinking to organize granular observations and takeaways to surface new patterns.

empty conference room with plenty of blank wall space. We spent the next few days sticking them up and moving them around in a search for common affinities and hidden patterns (see figure 3.5). This process is called *affinity mapping*.[8] It takes patience and some collective understanding from all team members to wait to speak on things until the process is complete. Under Bennett's tutelage, we were encouraged to do this silently between the individuals in a team (i.e., absolutely no talking). We sometimes played music or wore headphones to illicit a creative, meditative energy as we poured over the different Post-it notes of granular takeaways and observations. Some projects may require weeks of affinity mapping until the team is confident they've scoured through all the patterns and nuances. For Invoy, after about a week, we were able to make sense of things and comprehend where our investigations were taking us. We knew we were ready when the team started feeling excited about all the things we could pursue in reaction to what we heard, observed, and distilled in our synthesis. We could naturally feel new vectors emerging that would carry us forward though the forest of ambiguity with more confidence.

In affinity mapping, it's not uncommon to aggregate a few large clusters of Post-it notes as a signal of a theme's particular gravity (i.e., the quantity of Post-it notes in close proximity to each other) on the wall. Gravity suggests a key theme that we should prioritize in our problem-solving. We should also ensure that this grouping of Post-it notes is not just a bunch of takeaways that reinforce what we already know in terms of present consensus. If it is, we should move on and analyze the next grouping. But in my experience, a dominant cluster indicates that many folks voiced or projected a reinforcing perspective and that it's a serious point of commonality that should be given its due weight. What about the smaller clusters or single Post-it notes that may have seemed to be stranded on their own? Special attention should be paid to these as they might be less frequent but offer clues to a truly latent need affecting the person who voiced a concern or who projected a very unique feeling. Smaller signals on the extremes might be coming from early adopters who are positioned at the forefront of emerging trends and technologies. Their hacks to make this stuff work can be telling. These smaller signals might also come from laggards or folks who are choosing to opt out of the given topic or circumstance because of some other hidden reason that we need to uncover. From this affinity mapping exercise, we can surface major thematics or unique latent insights that come from the marginal extremes.

The next thing I typically do is try to indicate, on one slide, the top ten to fifteen insights that are interesting for an opportunity space that we are investigating. For each insight, I state what it is we are hearing, interpreting, or observing. Then, I usually accompany it with a supporting quote or a real observation from the codified research material. Finally, I might try to hypothesize the nature of opportunity that the latent insight is signaling for us. In other words, we're taking the liberty to frame a new vector that could lead us to potential solutions or new pathways of further investigation. At this stage, we should hypothesize the opportunity with an open aperture, and not immediately prescribe it or define it through the lens of our existing product or services. The material might point us somewhere new. If we look at everything through a conventional lens, we run the risk of ruling out an adjacent solution just because our business cannot yet rationalize how to make it work. At this point in time, just encourage yourself to simply cite the opportunity as fitting for anyone to take it on, be it your company, a competitor, or a new-to-the-world start-up. Let the vector breathe for now. Finally, whenever we refer to these top learnings, I often speak of them as *insight-opportunity pairings* (a term learned from Bennett) so that the team remembers them as critical vectors to inspire the work ahead.

As Bennett explained:

At the end of research, you have insights that lead to opportunities, right? . . . And I structure it that way. The reason why you do that is because it gives you the rationale for why you're pursuing a design direction. Every single time as students launch into ideation and concept development, they might not present the insight from the research that is leading them down that path. Because, if you don't remind people at every single presentation . . . if you don't say this is what we saw in the research and that's why we're doing this . . . if you don't say that, people will lose sight of why you're doing what you're doing, and then it becomes, "Well, I like the green one." [Laughs out loud.]

The lexicon [around this sequence] is important. You do your research . . . you have an observation in the research . . . which leads to the insight . . . which leads to the opportunity. And then, through ideation, leads to an idea. That's an unbreakable chain in my book. That's what I try to always use the same words you know . . . because I think it's a framework for discipline of language, which I think is important.[9]

Beyond these top ten to fifteen insight-opportunity pairings, there's usually a lot of other qualitative information left over that is valuable to organize and synthesize into more tools. There are a few places where this qualitative substance could enrich foundational anchors of understanding for downstream purposes. The first is building a richer understanding of our customers and key stakeholders. While the quantitative data and framing might provide a conclusive picture of key demographics and their attributes, we're still missing the richness of implicit behaviors, motivations, unmet aspirations, and attitudinal mindsets of real people doing real human things. Personas offer a means of synthesizing

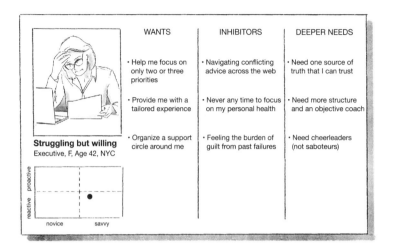

| | WANTS | INHIBITORS | DEEPER NEEDS |
|---|---|---|---|
| | · Help me focus on only two or three priorities | · Navigating conflicting advice across the web | · Need one source of truth that I can trust |
| | · Provide me with a tailored experience | · Never any time to focus on my personal health | · Need more structure and an objective coach |
| **Struggling but willing** Executive, F, Age 42, NYC | · Organize a support circle around me | · Feeling the burden of guilt from past failures | · Need cheerleaders (not saboteurs) |

**Figure 3.6**
An illustrative example of an attitudinal persona reflecting a target stakeholder's potential mindset, wants, inhibitors, and latent needs.

profiles to offer a reinforcing visual tool to remind us of the most important attitudinal mindsets within our target audiences. Figure 3.6 brings a very simple persona characterization to life. I believe that if we serve these personas, we'll naturally take care of the demographics that lie behind them that inform their context. A persona could actually be the profile of a real person we just talked to, someone extremely interesting and embodying a specific qualitative, attitudinal mindset among a group of critical mindsets that we deem important. It's great if this is the case, but it's not necessarily feasible at the same time. We may have to craft a representative caricature by piecing qualitative elements together that we heard or observed from multiple people, with the underlying quantitative data validating that this persona represents a significant swath of people.

Now, there is a lot of debate within qualitative research communities on the pros and cons of using personas. After I graduated from ArtCenter, Bennett invited me to come back and sit in on a few lectures with experts like Dennis Stefani (a longtime brand and consumer insights expert who led innovation campaigns at Added Value and Yamaha Motor Company), who crafted personas informed from a combination of rigorous quantitative surveying to size attitudinal niche segments and qualitative interviews that captured the thoughts of real people within those segments. I've personally seen where personas have been helpful to quickly snap the team into frames of reference around attitudinal mindsets, but I've also seen harm in what they tend to presume or potentially stereotype about people, especially if the underlying research was questionable at its foundation. A finite set of personas will have limitations in representing everyone or every belief system. To explore how to address this, I've been very intrigued by the work of Indi Young as I've combed over her latest book, *Time to Listen*.[10] Young encourages us to listen deeply to people by giving them space, and to really work hard to unpack their unique cognition and thinking styles around the specific purposes they are trying to accomplish. Indi and I originally met several years ago at a Design Management Institute (DMI) symposium that my team hosted at BCGDV in Manhattan Beach, California, and she graciously fielded my request to catch up and discuss her latest thinking on qualitative investigation.

I am an abductive thinker. I want to build knowledge about people who are trying to do something. Let's imagine someone jumping from one plane trying to catch their next plane. OK, there's a purpose. What's all the cognition that people have done in the past, because I only do listening sessions about people's cognition in the past. One of the things that's really different from marketing is that we're not interested in how people use a solution or their reaction. I don't care.

I want to get past those things. I want to know what went through your mind. What was your inner thinking? What were your emotional reactions? How did you make that decision? What personal role or guiding principle did you apply? How can I find those things out? . . . So I can begin to see (new opportunities) with different thinking styles . . . how the different philosophical approaches are.[11]

In one of her recent projects centered on air travel, Young conducted eight intensive studies on the purposes airline passengers have when they move about, and one of the four thinking styles that emerged from the research findings was "use my time wisely." Young reminded me that a deaf leisure traveler could share the same thinking style(s) as a jet-setting businessperson, so building knowledge based on people outright might not be as effective as unpacking the cognition around a specific purpose: help me save time! More people may share that same thinking style, and you might find bigger, cascading opportunities for engagement. Even better, by focusing on a thinking style, we can support a broader variety of people, not just the folks we believe we're serving from a narrow set of personas (or even worse, the archetype some teams have of their ordinary-average user that is held up as their standard far too often). Young believes that thinking styles can help get teams out of their previously held demographic assumptions and allow them the chance to measure against the bias that is already engrained that happens to reveal itself in their existing solutions. What excites me about Young's work is that it provides a purposeful set of new vectors to go deeper into the qualitative substance of cognition that drives people, and also gives us more ammunition to avoid simply coding our strategies from just the quantitative data. I love how Indi has really opened my aperture on appreciating people versus looking at them through a biased, product-centric lens.

If we keep pushing further along these lines of purpose and intention, the next logical place to synthesize qualitative findings could be through the lens of our customers' or stakeholders' journeys that illustrate their experience. We want to inventory the key happenings that occur over the course of time that's relevant to their thinking style or specific purpose. It's important to identify the thinking style or purpose for each journey map because different thinking styles will need different maps. Whether it's a day in a life, month in a life, or year in a life, we should inventory all observed realities for each thinking style. We need to inventory all of the significant ups and downs that were echoed in the research findings and take note of where our existing products and services intervene. We probably gleaned many takeaways that relate to them being either satisfied or frustrated with the range of tools they've been given. Friction can come in the form of pain points, frustrations, or potential latent needs waiting to be unlocked and understood. We should also watch out for key inflection points where there could potentially be a *moment of truth* for a brand to intersect and meet people where they are when it truly matters to them. We'll speak more about moments of truth later, but these points in the journey offer potential on-ramps for us to gain significant mindshare with the people we're serving. If we show up for people in a thoughtful manner, they will remember us for that and reward us with their repeated use of our product and eventually their loyalty.

Finally, we should recognize that our audiences never navigate their journey alone. There are other actors that likely have to be engaged in some way. If I'm a customer, I will bump into a salesperson. Salespeople have managers to report to, and so on. Thinking more systematically beyond the individual, we should spend bandwidth distilling the value criteria most important to each stakeholder and explore how value is exchanged between individuals in a system. How are people incentivized? Is it ethical? Will dominos fall when something breaks? My friend Sheryl Cababa (author of *Closing the Loop: Systems Thinking for Designers*) opened my eyes to the potential cascade of unintended consequences that stem from every design or business decision. We should even question our own positionality, power, and privilege as we interrogate systems. We can codify our learnings in the form of system maps and infographics. Other entities that we might document might include other elements that are nonhuman, such as algorithms and machines, instrumental in relaying, transmitting, and storing data or currency. Additional elements might include our environment, our neighborhood, and society at large, and we may need to comprehend the exchanges of value or resources that move between us and the larger ecology surrounding us. This raises the question of how we might highlight extraction and potential circularity. We have the opportunity to blend quantitative data and qualitative information to inform a new picture that disparate disciplines may not have had the benefit of seeing before. The power of a visual can speak a thousand words, and we should leverage data visualization and infographics to help surface the bigger message of how the pieces fit together and how value moves around.

Up until now, we've been talking a lot about research, both quantitative research to frame and qualitative design investigation to uncover the substance necessary to shape new ideas. Seeking understanding is a natural starting point for any curiosity. However, we need to be careful to not position our investigative efforts within someone's formulaic work plan. If you're part of an existing enterprise, ideas are already on the table. Recognize what's there. But keep an open aperture when it comes to spotting fresh inspiration and imagining more divergent vectors of exploration. Intuitively decide what information you allow to inform and color your research approach, balancing informed hypotheses with some breathing room to explore with an open mind. Also, we don't just have to plow forward interviewing people for weeks and weeks until we grant ourselves permission to react to what we're hearing and observing. Andy Ogden, chair of the graduate industrial design program at ArtCenter during my time of study, would remind us, "Don't forget to be the designer. You are the designer. Design." Therefore, as you're hearing or observing things in the field, pull out your sketchbook and scribble ideas. You don't even have to be a designer to do this. No matter your discipline, jot down the idea and tuck it away for later. Conversely, you don't have to stop talking to people either, even after you've synthesized a bunch of research findings. Keep in touch with your audience. Concept-test solutions with them. Keep them engaged as long as possible. If you find yourself having your runway for investigation threatened, cut off, or condensed, heed the following warning from Bennett:

> You must understand what's in the heart of your customer. If you don't know what drives them and what are their values, what are their beliefs . . . if you don't then you're likely not going to produce something that they would find useful or valuable.
>
> You know, some companies are in a position where they don't have to worry about that too much . . . they have been coasting along with some sort of legacy product that is selling itself. Most of the customers are if not happy, they accept it as expected performance. But companies like that will run the risk of some insurgent company coming out of left field that really understands what's making their customers tick and then the whole world will orient around that vision.

• • •

### Takeaways: Uncovering the Substance of Latent Insights

• Using quantitative framing for boundary conditions, consider different investigative approaches to find new vectors of exploration. At each milestone, pick the best approach that makes the most intuitive and logical sense based on the information you have available to inform the next step.

• Engage your target audience and key stakeholders with complete humility. The people you engage are not research subjects to be studied through a mirrored glass. They are not there to simply validate your hypothesis. Meet them where they are, listen, and really seek out what matters to them.

• As you synthesize research findings, build visual tools that encapsulate attitudinal mindsets, people's cognition around specific purposes, stakeholder journeys, and systems of value exchange to help the team understand new sources of latent insight and latent opportunity.

## 4 DESIGN IDEATION

SHAPING SUBSTANCE INTO CREATIVE SOLUTIONS.

Through qualitative investigation, we uncovered the rich substance that represents latent needs, core beliefs, attitudinal mindsets, and potential frictions affecting our target audiences. Through quantitative framing, we hopefully understand where it's best to spend our time in terms of high-priority audiences and key opportunity spaces within a dynamic market. With quantitative and qualitative research working in tandem, we have some anchors and material to work with as we navigate the forest of ambiguity in pursuit of innovation. Now it's time to discuss putting two and two together and generate some ideas. Granted, our ability to generate ideas doesn't have to follow a prescribed order—thus, the title of this book. We can use any information we have at our disposal to begin crafting new ideas and solutions. While navigating qualitative and quantitative investigations, designers on your team may have already started sketching potential solutions based on their observations. Let them and give them the space. Also, even when the team's work plan says the research phase is over, you can always keep talking with your target audience. Reality is never as clean as the work plan on a PowerPoint slide; it will feel more chicken-and-egg. Celebrate that. We don't have to wait for a linear sequence of activities to begin ideating or even designing. We don't have to wait to spark another round of conversation with our target audience. It's okay to swap sequences based on your gut and intuition. Give yourself the permission to do so because the more astute you are about the complexities in your reality, the better you'll navigate the forest of ambiguity.

If we view the uncovered substance from our audience engagement as a critical input, then how do we get started to shape new ideas and solutions? To design something, there's many different interpretations of what the design process represents. Design thinking practitioners typically point to the *double diamond approach* made popular by the UK's Design Council to describe the creative journey.[1] Through discovery (the first diamond), we diverge to cast the net wide and ensure we've investigated the extremes before converging on a specific opportunity. Then, through design ideation (the second diamond), we diverge and create a multitude of ideas before we turn that corner and converge toward a coherent, integrated solution against the opportunity in question. Others might show the design process as a linear series or a cyclical loop of steps that speak to discovery, developing ideas, prototyping, and testing to eventually rinse and repeat again as we learn. Frameworks like these are simplifying vehicles to help people understand the typical process a designer takes. However, there's a ton of nuance within most real-world circumstances. We just have to be careful to avoid taking these rubrics as formulaic mandates and mindlessly plow through a simple sequence of steps because we feel that to do so is to design or is the specific process we must follow. Before mapping a sequence of initial activities, let's first explore how to channel the substance from our investigations through three mental models that I am proposing to help us get more prepared and organized for ideation.

## CHANNEL INSIGHTS BY DIFFERENT SITUATIONAL CONTEXTS

When I reflect on my own professional experiences in leveraging design, the simple frameworks I've used tend to fall apart in the face of complexity or stakeholder scrutiny, forcing me and my teams to scramble to resolve the gaps. I'm not dismissing the original authors' intent and intelligence behind these frameworks when I say this; it's just that they tend to be abandoned in the face of real complexity. So we need to inject more care to appreciate complexity, nuance, intuition, and tactical ways to navigate into our creative problem-solving. Several years back, on a long-haul flight to Germany to give a keynote presentation, I pulled out my iPad and sketched an interpretation of the creative process (see figure 4.1) through the lenses of reality, nuance, and complexity. In my scribble, I blended the double diamond with cyclical rhythms and scribbles to convey the turbulence that we often encounter. From the fuzzy front end (i.e., the forest of ambiguity)

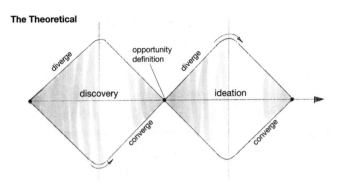

**The Theoretical**

**The Reality**

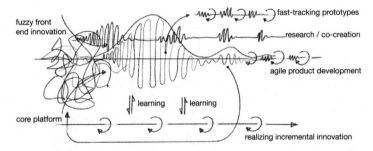

**Figure 4.1**
Kevin Bethune's personal scribble that visualizes the realities of the innovation journey versus the theoretical double diamond.

to potentially fast-tracking ideas right into prototyping, we have to understand the context of where we are and our ability to leverage creative problem-solving in those different situations. Are we ideating in blue-sky territory? Are we wrestling with the existing core platform and trying to accomplish incremental improvements (i.e., refinements)? Are we more downstream, and factoring in the latest uncovered insights as we prototype and test solutions? Situational context matters, and our approach needs to mirror that reality, balancing intuition with concrete steps of action.

## CHANNEL INSIGHTS BY DIFFERENT PROBLEM-SOLVING STYLES

The complexities of our time warrant teams becoming more multidisciplinary over time. I honestly believe that. However, every individual around the problem-solving table may see the path forward very differently. By precedent of their disciplines, their problem-solving styles may be different too. Business disciplines tend to skew toward hypothesis-first problem-solving. They will posit a "smart answer" and put it on the table early with a mindset of playing offense. "Let's go fast with an opportunity, until new data says otherwise." On the other hand, technologists may adopt a scientific approach, leveraging the research to frame experiments and define control groups to prove something. Designers may take a bit more time to pan for gold among disparate, granular insights. They hold off making assertions until they've had a chance to sort through their findings. Designers can surely make hypotheses too, but they typically allow things to simmer a bit before acting. In my experience, the best multidisciplinary teams take a moment to recognize their differences at the start and make each other aware of their norms and tendencies. It's actually a good thing that different folks around the table can evaluate insights through their own unique lenses. "I respect your hypothesis, but I want to spend some time investigating further before I can say that we're aligned." Embrace the differences here and give the team the space to consider different lenses on our potential vectors of exploration.

## CHANNEL INSIGHTS BY ORGANIZING CATEGORIES

Playing further on the panning for gold analogy, the substance we collect through our investigations is typically varied and nuanced. Some filtering, screening, and grouping will help us make sense of what we can learn just by organizing the substance in front of us. One helpful rubric I learned while under Katherine Bennett's instruction was the POEMS framework.[2] POEMS stands for the following categories: people, objects, environments, messages, and services (see figure 4.2). As we take the time to codify the research and affinity-map our Post-it notes to reveal patterns, we can run all the disparate data points, inspirations, and insights through the POEMS framework to add color around specific opportunities under each POEMS category. We can imagine how our research informs the relationships, dynamics, and value exchanges between people. We can think about physical objects and their place within an ecology. We can think about physical environments and spatial context as our stakeholders navigate their journey. In an information-rich world, we can think about the timing, placement, and relevance of specific messaging. Finally, we can imagine service opportunities as we might imagine ways to facilitate or deliver value across an ecology of different stakeholders. Organizing our substance into these high-level categories will ignite our brains to comprehend a new layer of thinking on top of what we already gathered.

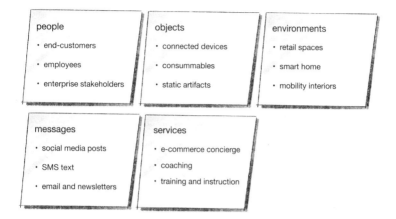

**Figure 4.2**
The POEMS (people, objects, environments, messages, and services) framework helps organize our research findings to reveal new patterns.

By now, we've gained an appreciation for defining opportunity spaces through quantitative framing, as well as unearthing the depth of substance necessary to shape ideas through qualitative design investigation. By channeling that quantitative framing and qualitative substance into different contexts, we can get the most out of our research findings to inform our different vectors of problem-solving. As we distribute the research findings across our multidisciplinary team, we need to anticipate how each discipline's precedent for problem-solving influences the work ahead, and we should strike a healthy balance across disciplines. We should avoid allowing one discipline's tendency to dominate the others and thus avoid the likelihood of having precedent keep us tracking along the wrong vector for too long. Finally, we can leverage frameworks like POEMS to organize our research and allow us to see it through the lens of purposeful categories that may offer clues pointing toward potential solutions downstream or may surface less-than-obvious patterns that simple categorizations might reveal.

Now, please remember that you can ideate at any time. You might already be the type to whip out your sketchbook and generate ideas. That's a great habit to have. But for most people, generating solutions from seemingly thin air may feel intimidating. I surely felt this way when I was just starting my professional journey in design. I honestly felt lost in a forest, sometimes paralyzed on how to even get started. Perhaps I doubted myself or felt unsure about taking the first step. However, I had to learn that you can look down at your feet and realize you probably have more information at your disposal than you know to inform a new vector of exploration. You have ingredients to leverage to do something—anything. You're also probably part of a team where you can collaborate with others to make that first step even smarter. You're hardly ever alone. If you listen further to that University of Pennsylvania talk from Denzel Washington, he encouraged those graduating students to "fall forward . . . at least [you] will see what [you are] going to hit." You have to try something new and see if it sticks. If it doesn't, at least you can learn why and have the opportunity to try again. Ideation is not for the faint of heart, but with the right mindset, you'll get better with practice. You'll also learn to avoid being disappointed when things don't work—and they surely won't. Just because an iteration may have failed, it doesn't mean you are the failure. You are not a reflection of your failures, and they surely do not define you. Keep going.

When you ideate, you're putting creativity in motion. You are fulfilling a special act of combining disparate information together in a new and novel way. As you get started in the ideation journey, think about how much effort is appropriate to put into your initial ideas. Gone are the days where we fielded a brief and were expected to go off into our cave for several weeks and come out the other side with a fully baked, beautifully designed solution. We can't design to a spec (a specification) anymore. The world is too fluid and will happily give us signals on whether an idea is good or not if we have our radar attuned to our audiences and have an open aperture to capture feedback. To *fall forward* means practicing failing by putting a lot of ideas out there quickly to test. Don't spend too much time on any one of them because most of them will surely fail. Part of your initial journey might be just practicing the mechanics of ideation like a warm-up exercise. We have to get the creative juices flowing before we even know where we are going. Creativity is the act of making natural sparks and connections among the substance of data, inspirations, and insights you have available to you. Make your best efforts to try piecing elements together to shape a new idea of possibility, and new vectors of further exploration will emerge. Trust yourself and go for it.

I want to offer an analogy on how this can progress. From my exposure to physics as a mechanical engineer, I remember how energy translates across an environment, as either light or sound. These types of energy sources travel in wavelengths, with a

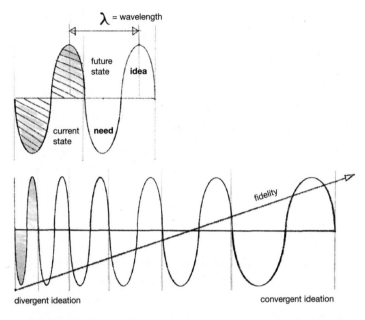

**Figure 4.3**
Lambda (i.e., wavelength) as a metaphor that lengthens from divergence to convergence with each passing iteration as you navigate the creative process.

particular amplitude and frequency as they travel forward through space. In physics, the Greek letter lambda ($\lambda$) is used to denote wavelength. I often think about using lambda analogously against the creative approach. Per figure 4.3, we should vacillate between (a) understanding our current-state realities, pain points, and frictions (the lower part of the wave) and (b) using the substance from our research to shape future-state ideas that make the situation better (the upper part of the wave). When we're early in our throes of ideation, lambda should be very short, with many waves occurring within a specific timeframe. We should move swiftly and create many fast ideas, exploring all the possibilities. We should sketch them with very little detail and resolution (i.e., low fidelity) so that we're not wasting time overinvesting in any one idea. This is where chicken scratch, thumbnail sketches, Post-it notes, and cartoon wireframes fill your desk or whiteboard. They should be easy enough to stick up in minutes and digestible enough to have someone stand up and share what they were thinking based on how they connected the dots among needs, inspirations, and potential solutions.

As you journey through your iterations and learn with every step, lambda should naturally lengthen. That translates to us investing more time, substance, and fidelity into some of our ideas. To flush out ideas to a level where they are rational, we have to spend more time on them. That also means having the discipline to stop progress on others in order to use the limited time we have wisely. Time is key, and time affords us the runway to shape more intuitive, thoughtful solutions. Often, too many teams go too fast on any and all ideas when lambda really needs to be lengthening on just a few. This is especially true for the ideas we start to believe in in terms of their potential downstream. It's at this time that we should have a mindset to slow down. Part of that involves picking which initial ideas deserve more thought and focus. We have to use some discernment to pick the ones that will matter, then invest in them accordingly. As we scan over our early ideas, are the ideas any good? Does this pile of sketches coincide with the value criteria of our stakeholders? How might they fall apart in the face of obstacles and major blockers affecting our industry? Does the idea lend potential to downstream differentiation and competitive advantage? We should consider these questions as we stop the progression of some ideas and lengthen the lambda for others.

Short lambda likely reflects a period of divergent ideation where we're just trying to fall forward for as many ideas as possible without too much judgment. Long lambda requires more effort and deeper thinking. As we start to bring in our discernment to pick into which among the early solutions we will invest more time, we'll begin the throes of convergent ideation as lambda lengthens. Let's discuss the intuitive discretion we can take during the throes of divergence followed by convergence, and sometimes vice versa, as our reality sometimes requires.

### DIVERGENT IDEATION

We talked about how ideation can feel intimidating for anyone. Well, in fact, the entire multidisciplinary team might feel a bit nervous to begin generating ideas. The spirit of divergent ideation is to push ourselves to create as many ideas as possible. This is the time to suspend disbelief and reserve judgment. You want everyone around the table feeling encouraged to create new ideas. The reality is that most will fail. That's okay. It's about casting the net wide and assuring ourselves that we explored all the possibilities and extremes. Though we come to the team room with our different problem-solving styles, together we can adopt a mindset of play and creative optimism. We should embrace the free spirit that is clearly evident in children and exemplified by their fearlessness. They cast inhibition aside for the fun of exploring. We might engage in brainstorming over Post-it notes, mind-map on the whiteboard, or invite each other to a *game storm* (i.e., a generative game that encourages making sparks and connections across different inputs such as personas, trends, and business models; see figure 4.4). You might slide a box full of knickknacks or LEGOs and see what the team can come up with as they take out the contents. Create an idea within a few minutes, then move on. Create another one. Move on.

Fostering divergence should happen at both an individual and a team level. For individuals, this is about getting yourself isolated from the team to create and explore ideas through your own individual thought process. As an industrial designer, I may quickly sketch a lot of small sketches (often called *thumbnails*) of a physical object I intend to design, with different quick silhouettes that serve as starting points for what it could look like with minimal effort. A few years back, I had an opportunity to design a cold-storage wallet in the form of a physical electronic device that needed to store cryptocurrencies and NFTs. We called it the Keevo Hardware Wallet.[3] You can see some of the many divergent sketches for that device in figure 4.5 (and the final result by skipping ahead to figure 6.2). The divergent sketches really helped the Keevo team consider all the possibilities before narrowing in on any one direction. We could use them to socialize with crypto enthusiasts to get feedback on many potential options we were considering. In the realm of digital products and services, I would

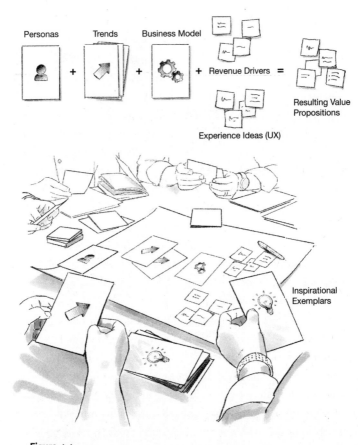

**Figure 4.4**
Game-storming exercises allow the team to create value propositions on the fly, leveraging a diverse assortment of inputs (e.g., personas, trends, business models, exemplars, revenue drivers, and UX ideas).

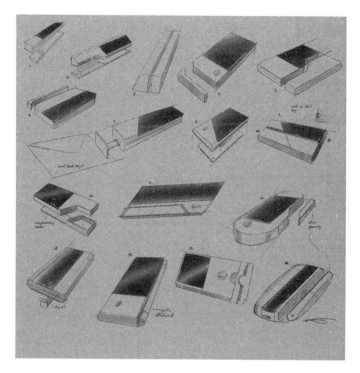

**Figure 4.5**
Divergent sketches of physical form factors to establish the initial
directions that led to the design of the Keevo Hardware Wallet.

expect a UX designer to pencil out many different potential user flows or low-fidelity wireframes to entertain a number of different ways to solve a problem. In either scenario, each individual has to push themselves to explore all the possibilities. Having inspirations nearby (mood boards, collages, real-life examples of analogous products or services, etc.) may help keep an individual inspired to continue sketching ideas.

At a team level, we should combine our brainpower and make as many ideas as possible in the same respect. Before beginning, we must encourage the team to embrace a "yes, and" (versus "yes, but") mindset. For any idea that's offered (no matter if it's a scribble on a Post-it or a low-fidelity wireframe), each person should acknowledge that idea as a valid contribution, and they should only seek to add to it with a new layer or thread of thoughtful contribution, versus judging or dismissing it. To help that along, introducing new ingredients from time to time can sometimes keep the brainstorming momentum alive. This can take the form of introducing additional exemplars, market paradigms, inspirations, and data points to help everyone easily find new anchors to inform and inspire even more ideas. Conversations that encourage "what if," "what about," and "how might we" questions will hopefully foster open-minded, exploratory conversations across the team to open up new doorways for exploring solutions. Through "yes and," we're allowing and empowering our teammates to conjure up more vectors. Through their divergent ideation, teams will create new pathways to advance along the nonlinear journey through that forest of ambiguity that persists whenever we're in the pursuit of innovation.

Beyond Post-it notes and additive conversations, we can leverage simple visual frameworks to provide our teams with a frame of reference as ideas continue to percolate. It could be as simple as writing a word on a whiteboard that relates to a potential solution and allowing the team to mind-map related, adjacent, and analogous ideas from there, creating several branches from the initial word. Another visual that may help is to characterize each stakeholder in the form of a day-in-a-life, week-in-a-life, month-in-a-life, or full-life journey that describes their phases and inflection points. We can pick a particular area of that journey and ask the team to generate ideas against that phase of experience, using it as a canvas to build ideas. It's important to note that I'm not talking about a market funnel characterized by the typical buying journey phases to have someone investigate, buy, and consume a product.[4] We should visualize the journey through the lens of our target audience and depict the nuances of their reality and intended purpose (my commute to work, my maternity experience nurturing a baby, my transition into retirement, etc.). Let's use that as a better canvas to seed our early ideas before we even attempt to rationalize our thinking through the construct of an existing business, marketing funnel, or product platform.

Alternatively, we could shake up our group's thinking by asking everyone to embrace different mindsets apart from our usual frames of reference. If we're a company operating within the industrial goods sector, we might imagine ourselves generating ideas as if we're Google or Meta entering that industry with the prowess of their technological advantages. What ideas would a tech company consider from the first round of ideas? How would those ideas change through a second round of brainstorming with the mindset of big tech? Within our given industry or market landscape, we could also adopt the mindset and attitude of our direct competitor. What would they do with our early ideas, and how might playing on their unique differentiation from us spark new thinking? Pushing further in the spirit of divergence, another set of mindsets we might garner comes from the work of Joseph Campbell, and specifically the eight character archetypes evident in the hero's journey: the hero, mentor, ally, herald, trickster, shapeshifter, guardian, and shadow.[5] Most storytelling narratives embody a combination of these characters in some way. What ideas would a ruler assert within an opportunity? How about a jester? How about a guardian, with ideas that characterize a brand having protective behaviors as it moves in the market? We can run our ideas through these archetypes to see how they contort and transform or spark more divergent ideas. These are just a few vectors one might consider among the hundreds of brainstorm techniques that people could use.

Once we get a handle on generating rough ideas, it's time to begin shaping them into divergent concepts that people can digest. I believe the best way to do that is to simply tell stories. A story includes a character that undergoes some type of story arc (e.g., a hero's journey), perhaps from a current-state reality to an idealized future state or an individual transformation thanks to an idea we introduce. We can make each stakeholder a character in a story that reflects the balance between their realities and future-state aspirations. We can write a short story about their potential experience, considering the rough ideas we have as inspiration.

We could enrich the story by surrounding the character's situation with trend-informed paradigms, headwinds, and tailwinds they may face as they engage our solution (see figure 4.6). We can turn this story concept into a visualized storyboard of cartoon frames in sequence like a comic book. My favorite stories to see happen when teams stay in analog mediums (e.g., paper and pencil) as long as possible as they sketch out characters and their plots on index cards. Much like a Hollywood editor, staying in storyboard format allows us to change the frames around at our leisure or (even better) to generate multiple storyline permutations.

There are usually two frames of reference for any story to work. Think of a stage in a playhouse. In front of the stage's curtain, actors perform the story and its plot in front of the audience. Behind the curtain, you have stagehands, lighting experts, audio engineers, and more, all making the story work, with a myriad of systems enabling the play to happen. We might think of a story, but we'll naturally want to think about what it will take to make that story work. What technologies will we need? What business mechanics will be necessary to allow different characters to exchange value with one another, which could be money, resources, or data? Beyond just the business concerns, what about the impact on the broader ecosystem? Those areas might be our neighborhood, broader society, the environment, social media, our local governments, data ethics, or regulatory boundaries. Through a systems-level understanding, we can sketch out the cascade of "behind the curtain" relationships, implications, and potential exchanges of value between characters. We can sketch out a system just as quickly as we can sketch a storyboard, with

**Figure 4.6**
A simple divergent concept storytelling template that can be easily filled in with Post-it notes and markers for ease of communicating new ideas.

simple visuals that allow us to identify the piece parts and interdependencies. We can provoke where we might affect relationships and create opportunities for new value creation.

In divergence, there's a lot of opportunities for the team to contribute regardless of discipline. Everyone can jot down their ideas on Post-it notes and generate a significant number of ideas if given the time. Anyone can chicken-scratch a storyboard of potential user experience. This can happen within the team room as a collective group or alone with an individual sitting at her desk to crank out her thoughts. When teams do have a designer included, divergence can get really interesting. Even though we're early in our ideation journey and the ideas tend to be expressed in very low fidelity, a designer can bring years of visualization experience to producing rapid-sketch contributions alongside their thinking. A picture speaks a thousand words. This will happen in the team room if the designer feels empowered to walk over to the whiteboard and contribute divergent ideas with rapid storyboards or system-level infographics. They can visualize and synthesize group conversations as well as seed their own ideas. Also, when away from the team room, it may make sense to pair a designer with a nondesigner to allow some one-on-one sparring and play on the different strengths of the designer and non-designer, respectively. This dynamic of leveraging designers at parity with other disciplines can accelerate our ability to create many ideas.

## CONVERGENT IDEATION

Once we've gathered a lot of early concepts and laid them out on the table, we are in a much better position versus starting from nothing. We can now turn a corner and converge toward the best ideas. We can use our skills of discernment and identify the strong parts of our divergent thinking that could be useful in weaving together a more coherent solution. We can assess the potential impact of specific ideas in terms of their likelihood to move the business goals forward. How does one concept help us foster growth or enhanced profitability versus another idea? How does another concept help us increase market share with our target audience versus another? What about the difficulty of executing one idea compared to another? Which is easier or harder to pull off? Within design thinking circles, these questions are answered by flushing out three primary considerations: desirability, viability, and feasibility (see figure 4.7).[6] By *desirability*, we mean: Do the convergent ideas actually matter to our stakeholders? By *viability*, we mean: Do the ideas actually help us make money and

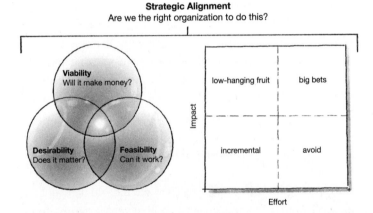

**Figure 4.7**
Convergent solutions require more discernment across a few dimensions (e.g., balancing desirability, business viability, and technical feasibility in parallel with impact versus effort) before we invest further in them.

give us some strategic or competitive advantage? By *feasibility*, we mean: Will the idea actually work in terms of the specific technical enablers required to bring it to fruition?

Similar to divergence, convergent ideation should happen at a team and at an individual level, requiring more delicate orchestration. As we turn that corner toward convergence, the stakes will feel higher because the team wants to feel like they are making good decisions in their design, business, and technology choices to rationalize a solution that makes the most sense. Perhaps the team can have a discussion around which ideas offer the most impact on target audiences in comparison to the perceived effort to pull it off. Per figure 4.7, we could model this with a two-by-two grid (i.e., impact versus effort) if we want and lay out our ideas on this canvas, but the conversation may also leverage gut and intuition based on our past experiences. We hopefully know our audiences compared to what our organization is capable of achieving. In terms of individual efforts, our business teammates can go model financial proformas of what our ideas might realize for the business if we successfully commercialize them. The product person can rationalize requirements, features, and the anticipated sequence of delivery. Technology or engineering teammates can investigate our back-end systems, prototyping capabilities, and existing intellectual property to assess a path forward toward feasible execution. The designer can design a coherent user experience to make the step-by-step interactions of the solution make sense to our target audiences.

Focusing on the designer for a moment, their iterations should feel complementary and intuitively connected to the work from other disciplines. How would this be accomplished? Pinning up a user flow of wireframes might strike the team as naive if the design has been explored completely in a vacuum. Therefore, I always advise my design teams to do more than simply pin up an iteration of their designs (a wireframe, an industrial design sketch, etc.). It's important to also surface the bullet points that explain why certain features and components are arranged the way they are in the converged solution's design proposal. Such an exercise is helpful as it allows the designer to speak to their design choices to reinforce collective understanding across the team. Even if the designer steps away, any other team member can look at the assets and understand why the iteration was shaped the way it was presented. Now, that may not be enough context in some cases. Sometimes folks, regardless of discipline, don't know where we are in the solution's progression. To remedy that, I recommend that the designer frame where we are in the process and what elevation of problem-solving (i.e., are we talking about the thirty-thousand-foot strategic level of thinking, or the details at ten thousand feet?) is appropriate for feedback collection. If a designer is wrestling with core information architecture, now is not the time to give feedback on the site's button color. That will come much later in the journey.

We should also consider prototyping our design proposal and putting it in the hands of our audience. This infers the need to test the rationale of what we're conceiving as a converged solution. Hopefully, we haven't shut off the conversation with our audiences that we previously engaged in our last rounds of research. By staying engaged, we have the opportunity to test our thinking by putting those prototypes in front of our target customers and stakeholders and eliciting honest feedback. In our desire to test, there's a risk that teams might behave transactionally here. They might illicit a conventional agency to test the solution with different customers. Often, the questions are biased, in the vein of, "Do you like this? . . . No? What would you change?" Or we can repeat some techniques like MaxDiff to compare the weighting of importance of a given set of feature sets under examination. What we miss here is the opportunity to empathize with an open aperture with our audience, even with a product prototype sitting in front of them. In my time at BCGDV, we would advocate for the right human-centric experts (e.g., strategic designers) to stay involved through the final paces of convergence before a product concept moved into its incubation (or build) phase. Even with a converged solution, there will always be gaps in understanding. We have to remain humble, especially in the final steps of convergence. Sometimes, the feedback might require blowing up a solution and starting over to find a new vector toward an even better solution. Allow it.

Even though we covered divergent and convergent ideation in their natural order with each other (much like the double diamond framework), reality always steps in to show us the opposite approach. Sometimes, in the throes of divergence, the business might stumble on an idea that really excites everyone and fits the capabilities of the business. That idea might be fast-tracked directly into a prototyping stage of work, leading to an immediate build of the actual product. The lenses from our discernment and success criteria need to be quickly applied in this case. For the business, skipping steps may be deemed acceptable because of the immediate context of business viability and the market urgency to strike while the iron is hot. In the throes of our convergence, we may stumble on a cognitive disconnect between our converged solution and what our target audience actually cares about. Somewhere, we may have missed a key assumption, a typical outcome whenever we're trying to create something new. We may need to circle back with our audience to learn more, reframe our initial brief with better knowledge, and repeat another round of divergence to explore more options before reconverging again toward something better. This can even happen when we're deep in the throes of agile product development, where something might break during our build, test, and learn cycles. We may have to alternate our divergence and convergence accordingly. It's messy. It will happen. Embrace it. Prepare for it.

• • •

### Takeaways: Shaping Substance into Creative Solutions
• Take some time to organize the substance uncovered from your research findings into different situational contexts, different problem-solving styles (hypothesis first, bottom up, or deductive), and different categorizations (e.g., with POEMS) to see what you have in new and interesting ways.
• Embrace divergent ideation to suspend judgment and create as many early ideas and rough concepts as possible. Divergence requires a mindset for failing early and often and can happen

effectively at the individual or team level. Defer judgment until you've exhausted all possibilities.

• Collect the best ideas from divergence and leverage convergent ideation to weave together the best solutioning. This is the time to leverage deductive thinking, discernment, and assessments of each solution's impact versus feasibility. Stay connected to your audiences and pivot as necessary.

## 5 DESIGNING MOMENTS OF TRUTH

SHOWING UP FOR PEOPLE WHEN IT MATTERS.

When we think about how we navigate our day-to-day experiences, there are some very unfortunate paradigms at play. If I open my smartphone in the morning, every social media app is full of advertisements marketing something to me. If I had a conversation with my friend yesterday about some product, my Instagram and X (formerly known as Twitter) feeds will be full of ads that stem from that conversation. I only need so much stuff. We are constantly bombarded with the lure to buy. I say this without judgment for anyone reading and reflecting on their own buying habits. But if we take a step back, we should evaluate our reality and the systems that inform it. My friend and mentor, John Maeda (vice president of engineering, computational design, and AI at Microsoft), often uses a computationally derived visual of an infinity loop he designed with actual code (see figure 5.1) in his presentations. We talked about this visual (at least my interpretation of it) during a video livestream together on LinkedIn, where I likened the infinity loop to the accelerating paradigm of "marketers marketing" and "consumers consuming," as depicted by the left loop and right loop, respectively.[1] As computation continues to accelerate, this paradigm will prove more harmful when we think about the perils that hyperconsumerism already brings to our economy, society, and planet.

Instead of following this rote pattern, how might we envision actually showing up for people when and where they need us the most? What are the vectors that will lead us to that place? Instead of being encouraged to buy things people don't need, how can we creatively and intuitively deliver what they do need? We can imagine a wide range of answers to that question. There is the often-referenced theory of Abraham Maslow's hierarchy of needs (see figure 5.2), which offers an organizing principle for the levels of what humans need and value. From the base of the pyramid all the way to the top, Maslow argues that we're on a journey toward self-actualization to fulfill our purpose and offer our best gifts to the world. Other scholars, like Pamela Rutledge, PhD, a professor of media psychology at Fielding Graduate University, have since argued that Maslow's hierarchy of needs lacks recognition of the critical roles that social connection and collaboration play in realizing those needs through the cultivation of relationships, validating competency, and promoting teamwork.[2] While folks continue to debate the merits or problems in Maslow's hierarchy of needs, at least we can agree on a couple things. Let's agree that we want

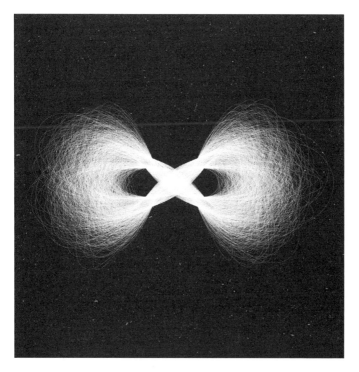

**Figure 5.1**
John Maeda's computational, artistic visualization of an infinity loop,
often used in his annual reports that speak to the dynamic nature of
design, business, technology, computation, resilience, and artificial
intelligence.

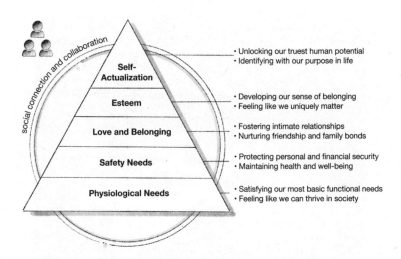

**Figure 5.2**
A visual of Maslow's hierarchy of needs, with an additional consideration for the roles that social connection and collaboration play for the benefit of individuals and their communities.

to point folks toward a trajectory to self-actualization and what that could mean in terms of the potential we could help unlock for them through the experiences we create. Let's also agree that the community around us plays an important role for us in fulfilling these needs. We need to show up for people in a way that fosters individual and collective growth.

I often wonder about which brands are actually showing up for people in meaningful ways beyond problematic consumption patterns. It's not easy actually when we stop to think about it. Which brands are tasteful about their marketing and not in our faces constantly until we think of them naturally or are referred to them at an appropriate time? Which brands encourage modest, sustainable consumption versus wanting the money grab and not caring about what goes in the landfill a couple years later? The first brand that comes to mind for me is Vitsœ, an iconic furnishings company based in the United Kingdom that ships modular furniture and shelving systems designed by Dieter Rams. Vitsœ credits its success to (1) really strong word of mouth, (2) its modular system that you can take with you (and further scale) upon a move to a new home or office, and (3) never needing to run a sale, ever. On the digital services side, brands like Uber and Airbnb stand out for me as they represent a person's ability to request on-demand assets that we don't need to own; the company doesn't need to own these assets either. They allow us to call up a car or book a temporary dwelling on our terms. There are still a lot of ethical, profitability, and operational questions for these digital services to address, but I don't see these platforms leaving us anytime soon. These exemplars may provide inspirational substance that can inform new vectors as we problem-solve in pursuit of innovation.

In the unique way that each brand shows up for me with relevant products and services, I usually don't think twice about using them again. In my own work at dreams • design + life, I pay particular attention to those opportunities that potentially foster a better way of showing up for people and communities. I try to prioritize our time for those projects that meet people where they are versus feeding into unsustainable cycles of consumption. The next sections discuss a couple qualities I tend to lean on that illuminate how brands might show up.

## UTILITY

When we design something new that captures someone's attention, what path of new utility are we actually creating for them?
What are we making that's actual useful for their needs? How
are we helping them complete a step that's naturally part of the
journey they want to fulfill? Can that step be accomplished faster,
better, and more meaningfully than the things they are already
doing today? Utility comes in many forms, and any discipline
might conceive of a useful idea or invention from their depth
of expertise. These contributions can come from engineering,
deep science, business, or design. The ability to feasibly deliver
new utility also depends a lot on timing. Certain variables (available capital, research and development, time to market, etc.) must
coalesce and converge to make a new form of utility even possible. Therefore, creating new utility correlates to our ability to
deliver meaningful innovations that are new, novel, and useful
in their introduction. Innovation depends on the context of the
situation, the proposed use cases, and the value that people see
in it within their lives. Ideally, they can begin to feel that when
we test our solutions with them. The value needs to be enough
to switch from the old thing that has worked to the new thing
that promises greater value, meaning, quality, time savings, and
functionality.

I often contemplate where this is occurring in my own journey.
What new utility have I enjoyed? As an industrial designer, I'm
sketching all the time, whether for product ideas or concepting
storyboards of potential user experience. I usually keep a stack of

fresh white paper, Copic markers, and ballpoint pens within easy reach. If a sketch comes to mind, I just reach for my materials and quickly do what I need to do. Granted, paper and pens are analog tools. However, it doesn't always make sense to use an analog approach, especially when I may need to share sketches electronically with other team members. I might also be on an airplane, where I can't pull out my analog tools as easily. In these scenarios, I tend to pick up my iPad Pro and my Apple Pencil. When I grab it, it just works without much extra thought. I don't have to keep pairing these devices together. I don't have to worry about charging the Apple Pencil as it sticks to and charges on the side of the iPad through a magnetic connection. The tablet knows when the pencil is engaged and ignores the touch of my fingers or palms. The amount of friction necessary to use it has improved considerably compared to when I used other drawing tablets in the past. That's a simple example of how Apple manifested utility for me as an individual and as a designer. How about for my business? Where do I see opportunity to unlock utility through the work of my practice?

I created dreams • design + life with the goal of working on holistic solutions that spanned physical, digital, and service-based affordances to unlock human potential. When it comes to creating new utility, I look for client partners primed to want to collaborate in that pursuit, using their intellectual property and enough foresight to believe they are ripe for the challenge of commercializing a new offering. Invoy was among the first of my client partners that fit this criteria. Thanks to Invoy's ingenuity and deep research in breath science, we could focus on optimizing the company's breath device to unlock the hidden insights in one's breath. Compare that to the alternatives. If you're like me, you probably have an ordinary bathroom scale at home. Even if I step on it daily, it may take me a couple weeks to understand if I'm actually losing weight due to fat burn, muscle gain, or water weight fluctuations. If I'm honest, I'm probably guessing when it comes to the balancing act between my diet and how many calories I'm burning through exercise over that same time period. I probably do a poor job of isolating the patterns. Other folks might go further by tracking their food intake with a food journal or a calorie-tracking app. Kudos to those folks who can establish the habit of jotting down what they consume at every meal. However, food journals are prone to error as there's risk of missing the small things we eat in between the big meals. And there are things we don't even think about and might not track, like the milk and sugar that goes into our coffee.

When I started to collaborate with Invoy, I joined its team in using the service (i.e., dogfooding). With Invoy, I wake up every morning and exhale into the breath device for a few seconds. Using the Invoy app, I answer a series of questions, reflecting on my behaviors over the past twenty-four hours, after which I allow the breath device to finish analyzing my breath sample. The app reveals a breath score at the end of the analysis (which takes no more than two minutes to finish). Later in the day, you can engage your Invoy program analyst through the chat feature in the app, and they will help you interpret your results and give you actionable recommendations that cut across diet, exercise, and many forms of habits. By breathing into the device every morning, I found myself empowered with a level of agency that I didn't have before. I wasn't guessing and trying to figure things out on my own. Through the utility of an intuitive breath device, a simple app, and a team waiting to help me, Invoy offered a perfect marriage of utility that was easy, painless, and eventually an essential habit for my morning routine. The first couple minutes of my morning is a moment of truth in a way. While using the Invoy platform, I felt my senses heighten to empathize with the experience of Invoy's members and really pressure-test the usefulness of certain affordances within their day-to-day routine. As obvious as it sounds, I could also use my own experience as a filtering mechanism to vet good or bad ideas for potential improvement of the platform.

## INFORMATION RELEVANCE

To understand any new form of utility we can bring to someone's journey, we also have to understand the full context of paradigms and realities they are experiencing. In the digital age, they likely have information impinging upon them in a million different directions. Ads are so pervasive, and new ads sprout up as soon as you search for or say anything, it seems. At times, it feels creepy that digital platforms are always listening or watching your every mouse click to infer something about you and what you might want to buy. The number of ads and the impinging information creates noise that commands a percentage of mindshare, whether conscious or subconscious. It's like the static you hear on a broken television. Brands have to fight through all of this to win attention. What if someone has an actual question that leads them to open up their device and enter a word in the search field? What they usually get back is a flood of prescriptive information before they find something that's actually relevant to their needs. With the infinite ocean that is the internet, finding what you need, when you need it is still a challenging endeavor. Time will tell if generative AI platforms like ChatGPT will come to the rescue. To give someone confidence that your new solution is appropriate for them, they need relevant information (benefits, reviews, ratings, etc.) to give them confidence that this utility is specifically for them and their needs.

A former colleague of mine at BCGDV, Ammon Haggerty (who's now serving as design cofounder at Joinable), had a knack for crafting design guiding principles and rubrics to help digital platforms better serve up relevant information that's actually helpful in the moments that matter. He led design for one of our ventures that eventually spun out of BCGDV—Formation, with Starbucks as Formation's first major enterprise client.[3] Starbucks wanted to invest in a new machine-learning platform that would drive advanced personalization, but the company was concerned about broaching the trust that it already had with a massive number of Starbucks consumers. In the context of our multidisciplinary team, we allowed designers a proper runway to come in and investigate the different value criteria across the mix of stakeholders. Haggerty's venture team eventually figured out a tactful personalization strategy that balanced privacy, trust, and progressive disclosure (i.e., progressive reveal of information distributed in limited amounts at appropriate times). This ensured that every consumer could enjoy benefits and offers that were served up only when it made sense to offer them based on appropriate context (geolocation, weather, preferences, etc.), customer permission, and the degree of trust afforded over time. Formation, recently acquired by BCG in 2022, was able to drive impact for millions of customers because of its tactful approach of serving up information and offers that would keep customers engaged.

If we think back to Invoy and its focus on the morning moment of truth, the new utility of a breath device requires enveloping that within a delicate orchestration of information that would give someone confidence that it's worthwhile to breathe into the device every morning. The Invoy team could easily overwhelm their members with all the data that was at their disposal from every breath test. Instead, Invoy's platform outputs a very simple breath score (on a scale of 0.0 to 15.0) that gives you a sense of whether you're burning fat, staying neutral, or storing fat. If the resulting breath score falls below 3.0, that means you are probably using different energy stores (e.g., glucose from carbohydrates) other than fat. That may or may not be fine, but at least you know what's exactly happening if you notice your weight trending up due to the likely storage of fat. If the breath score falls between 4.0 and 15.0, then you are surely using fat as an energy source and you should expect the fat composition in your body to decrease. Members can also step on a bathroom scale if they should so choose, but they have a better understanding of how fat burn is influencing the scale rather than reading the scale alone. With every handful of daily breath tests, you're bound to learn something new behind your scores and your program analyst's interpretation of them.

Seeing the breath score is one thing, but understanding what that means over the long term is another. There are a lot of variables at play in understanding what it means to manage weight. Many weight loss apps tend to throw a lot of data at us without necessarily helping to provide actionable insights. This unfortunate paradigm has been nicknamed the *quantified self*, a term made popular with the explosion of health trackers several years back. Invoy had to figure out how to reveal just enough information to get people comfortable with beginning an Invoy program. They start everyone with a virtual orientation session, with a real Invoy program analyst teaching each session. Then, new members have to test daily for fourteen days through what is called a *profile phase* to allow Invoy's platform to learn the metabolic characteristics of each individual. The member and analyst work together to then inform a weight-management program based on the profile phase, balancing meal principles, recommended habits, and accelerants such as exercise. The individual's food preferences and lifestyle also factor into the experience. Because life changes, so should one's program, and Invoy allows members to change their program every few weeks, balancing preferences with data-driven advice from the platform. Revealing informing progressively has helped Invoy retain its members longer than most weight-loss programs.

## EMOTIONAL RESONANCE

Assuming that we create a new utility that proves itself beneficial, that's great. To give someone confidence that the new utility is for them, we need relevant and succinct information that would provide them necessary context about the solution's fit for their needs. We have to earn their respect and trust that our brand deserves the right to belong within their preferred journey. How we show up matters. We had better be authentic when we do. Logic alone will not get us to that goal. While humans are surely an intelligent species, we're also a very emotional, irrational, and idiosyncratic one. We respond viscerally to how someone makes us feel, let alone how a brand makes us feel. If we as a brand enter someone's journey with empathy and compassion and navigate based on what's most appropriate for them, then we have a shot of making an impact. If we succeed in nailing a first moment of truth with that person, they may give us another opportunity . . . and another. After a while, we may establish a relationship based on trust, and consistent delivery of value for their needs cements that trust for life. Our brand might become a natural part of their subconsciousness in the sense that we seamlessly fit and that it would be hard to have another brand supplant that anchoring.

My friend Greg Hoffman (former CMO at Nike, Inc.) recently published a book, *Emotion by Design*.[4] In it, he shares winning strategies through the lens of his amazing creative leadership trajectory orchestrating the most celebrated athlete stories that helped make Nike so successful in the 2000s and 2010s. You can imagine that his teams had to build new brand campaigns on top of the existing juggernaut platform that was Nike, which had so many touchpoints already established across their core demographics. How hard it must have been for Hoffman and his team to keep the fire alive with each new story on top of the thousands that have already been told. Why should consumers care? From that level of play, Hoffman draws from his well of experiences and shares many toolkits that help new brands think about how they can cultivate a deep emotional resonance with their consumers. Almost like a stage director of a theatrical play, Hoffman encourages us to set a brand frame, strive for clarity, and take your consumers and stakeholders through an experience where you connect them to the aspirations and dreams they want to fulfill. Your brand should help them in that hero's quest (remembering Joseph Campbell) to help them feel transformed and empowered. Per Hoffman's wisdom, it's less about emphasizing what your specific product offering can do, but more: "What do we want this product to achieve? Not do, but achieve. What can it facilitate? How can it improve the [person]'s life? . . . Marketers too often lose sight of the purpose of their product by focusing on what it does. It has the latest tech, it has the best fabric it has the best engine, it has the best interface. These things might be true, but they say nothing to the person who really wants to understand something far more basic: How will this product help me?"[5]

Back to the Invoy example, which shows how the topics of weight loss and weight management are delicate and tricky to navigate. As I mentioned in the last chapter, even eliciting a conversation with someone about their weight raises all types of stigmas and emotions. Every one of us can probably identify a life stage in which we had difficulty managing our weight. In those moments, we probably felt like failures. The reality is that we were probably working with outdated tools, such as the bathroom scale or food journal. When we look at that number on the scale, we feel judged (see figure 5.3) and insecure. In reality, our weight challenges are

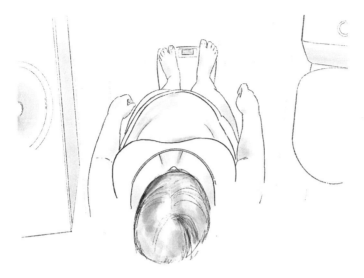

**Figure 5.3**
Stepping on an outdated bathroom scale can induce emotional feelings of judgment and an erosion of the hope that one's health trajectory might change.

not necessarily our fault as much as we are led to believe. As much as we try to be mindful and proactive with our habits, life happens to us. We might try to diet, but diet rules are often too rigid to account for, say, business trips that take us away from our routines, or we might find ourselves far away from appropriate foods to fit our programs. When seeking guidance on the internet, we have to navigate a ton of prescriptive information and are left without clear insights that relate to our circumstances. It's easy to be self-defeating, and hard to recognize that we're not the only responsible parties in the battle for our health. Invoy has worked hard to embrace these realities by studying the attitudinal mindsets and segments inherent in its membership community.

Invoy program analysts may have to engage with, for example, frontline employees who might be working two jobs to make ends meet for their families. They might only have the bandwidth to accommodate one habit change in their daily lives. Drinking water over soda may be a huge win for them when they probably can't spend time being overly picky about their food choices during a fast, twenty-minute lunch break. How can we show up and make things easy for them? Invoy may have to engage the office worker who struggled mightily in the past and felt like a failure, but is always willing to try new tools that offer a better promise. Deep down (and many members have said this), members recognize their need for structure and an objective coach, who can be a bit more data-driven than a cheerleader—not someone that will blame them for their missteps and make them feel worse. Program analysts must be objective with the data, providing clear facts about what's happening in each of their member's bodies, but they also need to be compassionate in the delivery of key insights and behavioral recommendations. A good coach never beats up someone who falls off track. They must affirm and encourage a member when that member is doing something right, and they must offer constructive guidance whenever there's a deviation. Add a healthy dose of empathy and compassion to be helpful, and that has garnered Invoy program analysts' success in building emotional resonance with Invoy's members over the long run.

Finding opportunities to shape moments of truth is not easy. From these stories, I hope you get a sense that a combination of serendipity, proactiveness, and market timing may be the variables manifesting together that allow an innovation to succeed. These are vectors we have to sense, spot, and anticipate in the forest of ambiguity. We have to anticipate which technologies and key differentiators are potentially ready for prime time and cultivated by the right team. I find myself constantly scanning for potential client partners who I feel are playing the long game in what they invest in for their future customer experiences, thinking beyond their short-term goals. Bullishly, I want to find those companies that are putting in the hard work to build differentiated capabilities and intellectual property that could be meaningfully leveraged in the future to inform a new experience. The vectors that lead to these opportunities are out there, but they will not find you: you have to put yourself in the forest and move about to increase the chances of finding them. Ideally, you talk with people in the know, scan market movements, and find vectors that will lead you to new signals. Signals lead to incredible opportunities if you keep scanning, exploring, and experimenting proactively.

• • •

### Takeaways: Showing Up When and Where It Matters

• Think about ways you might disrupt the current paradigm of marketers marketing and consumers consuming, only accelerated by the power of the digital world and AI. Think about how we can genuinely show up for individuals and communities in a truly humane and respectful way.

• Insert a new form of utility in the context of your customers' and stakeholders' journeys and do it on their terms. Try to boil down the new experience as a moment of truth that meaningfully intersects with them in an extraordinary, yet natural and intuitive way that makes sense for them.

• Think through the role that information plays to give people confidence to use that new form of utility you've created for them. Also, don't forget the role that human emotion plays. How you show up and how you make someone feel definitely set an experience apart from many others.

## 6 DESIGN INGREDIENTS

FULLY ENGAGING OUR SENSES.

When I was with BCGDV, our innovation work afforded us the chance to visit the MIT Media Lab at the Massachusetts Institute of Technology (MIT) from time to time. Member companies of the MIT Media Lab are able to tour the different research programs during their "demo days." I remember feeling intrigued by what the future could hold as most research programs forecasted or speculated what was plausible to see in the market in roughly five to seven years' time. Technologies like 3-D printing and touchscreens originally came out of MIT Media Lab. The research program that was my favorite to visit was the Tangible Media Group, led by Hiroshi Ishii, PhD. As we navigate the internet and mobile computing, most digital experiences are visually represented as illuminated pixels trapped behind a window of glass. As we navigate our physical world, we touch and engage physical material embodied as "frozen physical atoms," as Ishii describes it. Through speculative exploration, the Tangible Media Group has blurred the lines between digital and physical by giving physical material the computational power to transform itself, or digital material physical-like properties. This came to life for me when a researcher "poured" digital pixels into my hand (via projection mapping) only to have these pixels spill onto a table's surface below thanks to gravity, or when watching physical atoms transform their configuration through the group's inFORM interactive table (see figure 6.1). Demonstrations like this provoke the need to open our aperture beyond convention to imagine what ingredients we might use in our design work.

When I step away from such an inspiring environment as the MIT Media Lab, the conventions of my reality are noticeably more evident by comparison. I reenter a familiar world divided by glass screens. On the physical side, I navigate tangible environments inclusive of home, my workplaces, the objects within them, and perhaps the car I drive to get to and from those spaces. On the digital side, I navigate familiar patterns of digital interfaces in the form of websites, mobile apps, cloud-based services, and streamed media. As much as the pixels behind each screen might compel me, I find myself rubbing my eyes after a while to fight the strain. It doesn't feel natural to my eyes in the same way as exploring a sprawling forest on a nature hike. Shifting from the literal forest to the analogous forest of ambiguity, when I'm working on innovation, it should feel like I could discover something new and

**Figure 6.1**
The inFORM interactive table demonstrates physical-digital telepresence as a part of the Tangible Media Group's research at MIT Media Lab. *Source:* Tangible Media Group, MIT Media Lab.

interesting at any moment. That sense of wonder should permeate into what I could potentially create or what my team could create. We should feel comfortable being uncomfortable about what we might conceive that can play on all of our senses and match human intuition in the most thoughtful way, versus constraining us to convention. But during the act of creation, sometimes the forces of precedent snap us back into man-made expectations of what is considered familiar. When I feel this happening, are we pushing hard enough?

When we're charged with coming up with a solution to answer a need, there might be a premature tendency to rationalize new ideas through a conventional lens based on our current familiarity with existing products. This tendency is very real if you're working within an established brand known for shipping certain types of products and services. We may interpret an idea through the lens of manifesting it in the format of what has been sold before (a website, an app, a pair of shoes, etc.). Let's remember the POEMS framework introduced previously, which we can use to organize our observations during investigation or our ideas during ideation. The organizing categories of people, objects, environments, messages, and/or services could help us avoid snapping into a digital-only or physical-only mentality and remind us that these POEMS elements can easily cut across physical, digital, and service-related boundaries to fulfill themselves. These elements could have a role regardless of whether it's through pixels, physical atoms, or people. This gets even more interesting when you add in the growing power of AI to further blur the lines. An AI could emulate a person's role (automating routine tasks at scale), breathe new life into a connected object, or fulfill the role of messenger and service provider altogether. Part of veering off the trodden path is purposely dissolving the boundaries of conventional product constructs to imagine a more seamless and intuitive way of creating a holistic experience using all the ingredients we have at our disposal.

## SKEWED PARADIGMS

At the same time, we have to be cognizant of a few paradigms that indirectly hold us back from achieving this. "Software eats the world" has been a popular adage in recent years, coined by Marc Andreessen, cofounder of Andreessen Horowitz, a popular venture capital firm.[1] There's a degree of truth in this saying as physical assets continue to decouple from singular ownership, and media moves from in-person spaces (i.e., a movie theater) to being streamed over the internet right into your home or mobile device. You can call up anything on demand these days, whether it be your Uber ride or food via DoorDash. Artificial intelligence and automation further power and accelerate these services at break-neck speed. Thanks to the scale achieved by the FAANG companies (i.e., Facebook [now Meta], Apple, Amazon, Netflix, and Google [now Alphabet]) serving millions, if not billions of people, the appetite for digital software is enormous and will continue to grow. As expected, venture capitalists expect a significant return on their investments. Software brings them remarkable value, and does so fast, a lot faster than physical products and human services alone. Where start-up founders and enterprises place their value can easily skew prioritization of digital pixels over physical atoms. Thus, our businesses' attention spans may shorten to salivate over the returns that come from software and potentially shun investing in the physical side of things.

If we also think about the constantly accelerating flywheel of ecommerce, we can quickly lose a sense of humanity within our everyday interactions. When you need to call customer support for any issue, are you greeted by a person or by a touch-tone, menu-driven system that makes you want to scream because none of the choices match your specific question? When we're online, most e-commerce websites now have a floating icon of a support person wearing a mic. If you click it, are you going to chat with a real person? Probably not. Usually it's a bot, and you have to navigate several steps or unwelcome, prescriptive FAQs before you actually get to a real person on the other side of the chat. These moments add friction to our experiences and feed into feelings of digital toxicity or isolation. I take notice of brands that at least short-cut me to a human more swiftly. American Express Business Platinum has been a notable standout, in that every time I've needed to call them, I get someone very friendly who's always happy to help me with my specific requests, such as building a multi-city travel itinerary from my always complicated travel schedule. Loyalty card programs for hotels, credit cards, or airlines tend to short-cut me to a real human faster than if I didn't have a loyalty connection at all. I keep using them with the solace of knowing that a real human is only a couple steps away. I might pay a little more for a service with the security that I can reach a human being if needed than save a little now and risk paying for it dearly in a situation where I might have no access to support at all.

Those in older generations may remember the corner store down the street, their favorite restaurant around the corner, or their favorite tailor or dry cleaner. You were probably on a first-name basis with those business owners. Your loyalty was rewarded with exceptional service. These owners were masters of their domain: they delivered quality service and you could count on them for your needs. You weren't alone in this feeling. Your neighborhood vouched for them. The warm smile, the attentiveness, being handed your goods from around the counter . . . all of these moments mattered as ingredients to a very satisfying experience. The maligned incentives that come with our pursuit of scale and financial returns have skewed our ability to maintain this level of relationship or connection between brands and consumers, for the sake of growth and the spoils that come from unsustainable consumption. I might be able to have a fresh coffee delivered to me in minutes, but I can almost guarantee the quality and satisfaction will not be the same as I get during the ritual of taking a friend for coffee at a trusted establishment in my neighborhood. I feel that I'm not alone in this feeling. Are we approaching an inflection point where we can begin to appreciate the small, "slow" business again that does one thing extremely well and delivers service at an impeccable level? Let's not allow our boldness to innovate seamless, holistic experiences be thwarted by the never-ending digital chase for scale or returns. Let's ensure we find the right ingredients that tap into what makes us human and slow ourselves down to ensure we have the ability to deliver something special.

## EMBODIMENTS AND KENYA HARA

One designer who really shook my view of what design can do with its ingredients is Kenya Hara, a Japanese-born designer, curator, and writer. Hara has served as MUJI's art director since 2001 and spends his time primarily in academia these days. I discovered his writings in the wake of John Maeda's influence on me over the years. Many of Hara's works have recently been translated to English, opening a doorway that has helped me understand a radically different set of creative philosophies for how to understand the world and our creative opportunities within it. The first book I read by Hara was *Designing Design*, a masterful work of curated stories that offer a frame for how we might tap into our senses as we shape new experiences.[2] Hara didn't speak literally in terms of placating the obvious senses of sight, taste, touch, smell, and hearing. In a way, his work achieves a significant level of abstraction and a reframing of how these elements might reseat themselves. Hara's writings tap into what makes us human in a sensitive, intuitive, and almost subconscious manner, and it comes across through curated case studies that embody branding, environmental design, and specific product design work that spans physical, digital, and services. Hara's other books include *Ex-formation* (an exploration of "how little we know") and *White* (an investigation of abstractions taken from empty negative space), which tap deeply into our senses and reimagine how we interpret them. I am a big fan of his fresh perspectives on creativity.

Hara's books led me to study the works of industrial designers Naoto Fukasawa and Jasper Morrison, who carry forward similar sensibilities in their work. Fukasawa is a Japanese industrial designer, author, and educator, presently working in the fields of product and furniture design. You can find his industrial design product informing the lines at MUJI, Herman Miller, Alessi, B&B Italia, Magis, and HAY. Morrison is an English product and furniture designer who has also closely collaborated with MUJI, informing a wide variety of products ranging from housewares to environmental architecture. His work embodies a simple, minimalistic sensibility that results in truly honest products that are there for you when you need them. He's now the lead designer at boutique Swiss consumer electronics company Punkt., known for its hyperminimalistic mobile phones, the MP01 and MP02. Morrison and Fukasawa curated the Super Normal exhibition in 2006, where they presented two hundred ordinary or anonymously designed products devoid of branding and extra fluff. Their curation brought to life speculation on what defines or constitutes a "good object." Though seemingly unremarkable, many of the products you could foresee becoming better with time (i.e., sustainable, always useful), and they fit into our context so well that they almost appeared ambivalent or invisible. There's a beautiful set of tensions between normal and exceptional across the pieces, documented in the book *Super Normal*.[3]

Coming across Hara's work and the work of the esteemed creatives within his close circle really helped increase my sensitivity as a designer. This is why I wanted to spend a moment to shine a light on him and open our aperture on how we think about ingredients for design. He offered a different sphere of perspective that perhaps I didn't have exposure to from my creative foundation, which had its basis primarily in Western or Eurocentric pedagogies. That feeling of encountering such a new and fresh perspective really excited me as I dove into the readings—not only because of Hara's perspectives, but also as a strong reminder that there's a myriad of other perspectives around the world that are waiting to be uncovered. At least Hara's work shows us that we can be sensitive, thoughtful, intuitive, and bold at the same time. As humans are physical, sensorial creatures navigating a converging world of digital pixels and frozen physical atoms, where can we see the potential for seamless, holistic experiences that blur the boundaries? Due to existing precedents and convention, few enterprises exhibit the boldness to go after these opportunities. Apple, Google, connected-hardware pioneers like Tony Fadell, and start-ups like Rabbit (and its new "R1" AI powered gadget[4]) may be the most bullish. I want to see more enterprises and start-ups being bold in this regard to figure out the most seamless ways to show up for people using the full plethora of ingredients at their disposal.

## DILEMMAS IN PHYSICALITY

Now, before we get inspired to re-embrace the physical realm, we need to honestly reckon with the unfortunate challenges that have occurred in our efforts to design and create with physical material. Thanks to rampant industrialization since the beginning of the twentieth century, our lands and oceans are beleaguered by overwhelming pollution that comes from hyperconsumption and wasteful practices. The invention of plastic would ultimately become our curse as we can't walk a few yards without stumbling across plastic litter in our environment. Medical experts are even finding microscopic traces of plastic in our bodies thanks to the ill effects of unchecked industrialization. Modern science will have to continue to work hard to unpack how our precedent of mass consumption is harming us and our environment, and hopefully find ways to reverse course. As an industrial designer tasked with bringing next-gen products to reality, I should be extremely mindful of these precedents and the potential for harm before I create anything new. Every physical design should have a strong rationale as to why it should exist. This is not just to satisfy our own consciousness; we also have to anticipate new generations of consumers who will want to understand the ecological footprint and sustainability approach behind anything they purchase. They will align with brands who share their values in this regard. Sustainability needs to be a critical part of any problem-solving, full stop.

For a physical product to be deemed viable and worth the investment, it should satisfy more value criteria than before. First, there is the chord of *sustainability* that we just hit on, which we must treat as a given requirement before proceeding further. Second, it obviously has to fulfill its goals of *utility* and *functionality* in the context in which a physical affordance is absolutely necessary. Third, it should be a physical extension of the *brand promise* as a key affordance in an ecology that will now usually entail digital elements, copywriting, service protocols, and perhaps rich media content to complete the full picture of a brand's promise. It should amplify the brand ideals even if it's a static object fulfilling a singular purpose. It should speak on behalf of the brand that was responsible for its creation and serve in alignment with the values and needs of the consumer that purchased it. Even the static, lifeless shelves that Vitsœ sells tell a much bigger story in this regard than that of merely holding up your books. The company has a fan base because of the story and visual satisfaction its iconic shelves exude. They serve as a canvas for the personality of objects on your wall. Finally, digitally connected, physical objects have the extra challenge of *bridging* digital interaction with physical sense-making or effecting (i.e., generating a communicating output signal). A connected object may be the critical anchor in our ability to realize a moment of truth where utility, information relevance, and emotional resonance all work in concert together.

Before, I alluded to software commanding outsized and quicker returns than investing in physical product alone. Physical product creation lead times require serious consideration of pros and cons compared to coding software. When considering an innovation opportunity that could involve physicality, many venture capitalists have said to me that "physical product is hard." Coming from largely a physical product creation background, from my nuclear power days at Westinghouse Electric Company to my time at Nike, I understand how truly hard a physical product is to achieve. But with all variables considered, it may still be worthwhile to pursue a physical product in order to respond to a customer need with an intuitive, sensorial solution. The physical affordance might help make the digital service stickier and more relevant, helping to balance out the rationale for investment versus expected returns. Making physical stuff absolutely takes longer than coding software. From my time within Nike global footwear, the average time it took to rationalize a new footwear design from ideation to final confirmed sales sample took upward of twelve to eighteen months, depending on the design's complexity. Add to that another roughly six months of supply chain testing, gradating different shoe sizes, cutting molds for midsoles and outsoles, production trials, and more before the shoe ends up being available for purchase.

The aforementioned Keevo Hardware Wallet project is another concrete example. The Silicon Valley–based founding team had the foresight to know that a cold-storage wallet was absolutely needed to present a secure, multifactor authentication solution that could allow users to interact in different cryptocurrency exchanges and simply unplug from the cloud via our physical cold-storage wallet design. This offered what is called *air-gapped protection* from nefarious actors by inhibiting their ability to gain access to someone's assets. I was brought in to serve as a cofounder and as the industrial designer to lead the design of the device (see figure 6.2), permanent case, and outer packaging. It took us roughly eighteen months to get a prototype we felt good about before moving forward into production, and another six months to sort out contract manufacturing and the supply chain to necessary to assemble them in Southern California under our careful watch. Any mistakes on the physical design (a dimension here, a tolerance there) would be costly prohibitive errors to make, so we had to be very careful with our accuracy. This strategy required bold vision from the founding team's leadership to want to invest in the long lead time for the device, case, and packaging components, while being able to iterate the software side of the experience multiple times over during that same period. It wasn't for the faint of heart, but we reached an integrated solution that hinged on the device serving as a critical anchor. You can find out more about the Keevo design journey in a video I uploaded to YouTube.[5]

**Figure 6.2**
The Keevo Hardware Wallet—a cryptocurrency and NFT cold-storage device.

Some concepts might require even more foresight to imagine the feasibility of their creation. This is surely the case with newly emerging technologies for which we need to forecast when they might be viable over some plausible future timeline. My company had the opportunity to serve a prominent XR (i.e., mixed reality) company, and we had to respect the difficult confluence of shrinking battery potential, demanding power requirements, precise optic capabilities, and connectivity requirements that would inform its roadmap of products and investigate whether the result would be deemed viable by the stakeholders that might use the platform. It was a very cool collaboration to try to line up those stakeholder needs to help the company optimize how it might show up with its next-gen product. At the same time, we gained a very deep appreciation for the extensive foresight the company had to invest over many years (well before our project intervention) to ensure it would be viable to deliver at the appropriate time. Those deep investments were no guarantee for success. The journey was a long one of balancing calculated risk and reward while having faith the company could show up with relevant products against emerging needs in the landscape. With the advent of the metaverse showing up in all kinds of applications from gaming to architecture, NFTs, and transmedia-rich branded experiences, I suspect the company's gambles will pay off to match the needs waiting for us over the horizon.

No matter the ingredients we use, we have to remember that design represents an important capability that should advocate for what will make the most humane, empathic, and intuitive experience.

How are we arranging available ingredients to provide a path of new utility? In an information-rich world, how are we using the ingredients from content, data, and qualitative information as a means to convey relevant insight to give someone the confidence to use the path we've afforded them? How is our arrangement of ingredients (physical, digital, radical atoms, content, services, etc.) helping us show up for people when they might need us the most? To this effect, I'm especially drawn to the work of my dear friend, artist, author, and designer Jessica Helfand. In her book *Design: The Invention of Desire*, she reminds us that design represents a "intrinsically humanist discipline, tethered to the very core of why we exist."[6] Jessica takes the reader on very thoughtful journey of exploring our feelings, motivations, behaviors, and the resulting implications as they relate to our human condition. She adds a rich fidelity to our understanding of human needs and provides us with a looking glass to delve into the human experience. If we open our aperture to appreciate the full range of ingredients at our disposal, our boldness to push for the most intuitive, seamless, and thoughtful experience will surely be rewarded by those audiences we hope to serve.

• • •

### Takeaways: Fully Engaging Our Senses
• Question digital convention and the direction of any digital agenda. The speed of the digital clock may feel like an implied authority. Remember that software is just one ingredient at our disposal, and that we should speak up and check its power to ensure we show up for people holistically.

• Appreciate that humans are sensorial, idiosyncratic, complicated beings navigating a physical, complex, and always converging world. Digital alone will not satiate all of our desires and ambitions. Design boldly, sometimes slowly, to leverage the full range of available design ingredients.

• While we have an opportunity to converge physical atoms with digital pixels in new ways, we must remain mindful of the impact that making physical goods will have on our environment and consumption patterns. Every new physical affordance should have a strong *why* behind its existence.

## 7  FLYWHEEL EFFECTS

FINDING ACCELERANTS FOR OUR AIMS.

In our pursuit of innovation, navigating the forest of ambiguity is no easy endeavor. If it was, every start-up and every enterprise would be claiming far more progress on their innovation initiatives than what we hear about. Failure or *falling forward* is part of the deal. There's inherent risk and reward in the journey, but hopefully our efforts will lead us to a new place where we can serve our audiences in profoundly meaningful ways. To do so, we have to get comfortable getting uncomfortable so that we can learn as much as we can and find ways to challenge the status quo. Getting uncomfortable actually forces us to widen our aperture and stretch our muscles for creativity. Also, navigating doesn't always involve forward movement as a measure of progress. Finding success with innovation involves timing to a large degree.

Uncertainty and serendipity are very real variables as we navigate. Sometimes you and your teams might be on to a winning concept, but the underlying technology or the nature of market conditions isn't quite ready for prime time. Navigating may require you to be patient and sit still until some paradigm, trend, or technology materializes, and perhaps you have to do what you can in parallel to make sure other variables are in place for when that pivotal day comes. Waiting and observing the signals are nonlinear acts when the world tells you something's wrong if you're not always moving forward under some preconceived definition of progress.

Where can we draw in inspiration to embrace nonlinearity in our approach? I believe design serves as an important catalyst in bringing this about. When design is positioned at parity with other disciplines around the problem-solving table, the team will gain nonlinear advantages thanks to design's innate sense of human-centricity and future foresight. Design must really evangelize for people and anticipate their needs when and where it will matter, which is usually at some confluence of factors that will inform our audience's future experience. Of course, our teams can't materialize a solution instantly against an identified need. Relevant solutions take time to create, so we must anticipate how we can best show up and be prepared well ahead of our present moment. Design must help the multidisciplinary team follow suit in doing the same. The team should learn to anticipate where things are headed and figure out what story they want to make real. If design plays too small, then linear, formulaic precedents could seep back into the team's approach, stymieing meaningful progress toward the *right* solution versus just *any* solution. Figure 7.1 illustrates

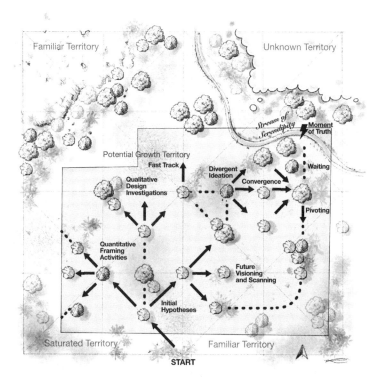

**Figure 7.1**

Navigating the innovation journey through the forest of ambiguity, while leveraging design's nuances and complexities to steer accordingly.

what navigating the forest of ambiguity can feel like when we consider the choices that design can help inform. It's about taking the most intuitive step forward and leaning on design's nuances and complexities to guide our path.

No matter how nonlinearly the innovation journey plays out, there will always be circumstances that can get in the way of progress. From a people standpoint, you might not have full multidisciplinary representation across design, business, and technology. How might you overcome this gap? Maybe you're part of a start-up. Each member of the founding team usually has to wear several hats to round out all disciplines. If design is completely absent in this team, how might you seek out design expertise from advisors or freelancers and include their voice in your approach? If you actually have designers within the team, are they fully empowered to operate as equal contributors alongside people from other disciplines? In both instances, can the team truly embrace design's nuances and complexities, or do you suspect they are locked into one dominant approach or line of thinking based on traditional precedents? In terms of the nature of the business itself, maybe you don't have the bandwidth to spend enough time on innovation due to other priorities. This may be due to the normal blocking and tackling that you have to do to keep the business running. You do what you have to do. However, this will quickly turn into an obstacle preventing you from preparing adequately for future needs and future-proofing your relevance to the audiences you claim to serve.

In my experience navigating different innovation endeavors over the years, there are some phenomena to be cognizant of and specific variables at your disposal that can serve as accelerants for your aims. If we choose not to address them, we'll make ourselves vulnerable to potentially negative phenomena that will inhibit our innovation journey and hurt our future relevance. One analogy that comes to mind from my mechanical engineering experience is the notion of flywheels. A *mechanical flywheel* is a heavy wheel that is attached to a rotating shaft that is integral to a pump or a motor assembly. Its heavy mass provides rotational momentum to balance out any volatility in the forces and speed inherent in the running system. If the engine sputters or loses power momentarily, the flywheel's momentum will keep the shaft spinning and the system in balance. The business world also speaks of flywheels. Jim Collins, author of the best-seller *Good to Great*, speaks of *flywheels* as small wins for your business that build on each other over time, where the compounding momentum carries the business forward almost by itself.[1] In my experience, there are five unique accelerants that apply to innovation that I believe help increase our momentum when navigating through that forest of ambiguity. Let's look at them one at a time.

## GUIDING PRINCIPLES FOR DESIGN

As we touched on before, it's not enough for us to stick our work up on the wall when sharing ideas. Instead, we should always be ready to offer an explanation of the *why* alongside the iteration or sketch. If we're designing a website, each wireframe we stick up on the wall should have callouts that explain what we're trying to accomplish (see figure 7.2). Each element of the expressed

**UX Landing Page Wireframe**

**Design Guiding Principles**

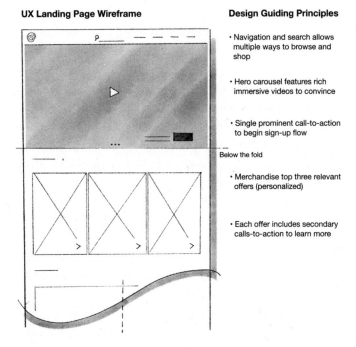

- Navigation and search allows multiple ways to browse and shop

- Hero carousel features rich immersive videos to convince

- Single prominent call-to-action to begin sign-up flow

Below the fold

- Merchandise top three relevant offers (personalized)

- Each offer includes secondary calls-to-action to learn more

**Figure 7.2**
UX guiding principles for design for an illustrative website landing page.

idea should have a logical reason for being, and this can be true from the low-fidelity iterations of divergence to the richer-fidelity iterations as we converge. If the business needs to acquire fifty thousand customers over the next quarter, then this landing page should do a great job of attracting, informing, and convincing would-be visitors to actually consider becoming customers. The bullet points should speak to what each section of experience is accomplishing. "Here [literally pointing] are places where the CTA [call-to-action] buttons need to be prominent. Here is where we quickly articulate the value proposition in three digestible steps to convince someone that we can answer their need. Here is where we encourage them to take the next step with a clear benefit statement of what awaits on the other side of that potential click. Here is where we are asking for information from them, with a clear statement of the benefit they will get by providing such information." As we huddle around the wireframe to critique it, ideally we're critiquing the *why* alongside the composition of the sketched visuals.

The opposite of having guiding principles is obviously not having them. That is a painful situation in which to find yourself, and I say that candidly from experience. When you have to defend your team's design decisions in front of key stakeholders who could decide to sponsor or sink the project, you ought to have your design "cheat sheet" in hand. There's nothing more unsettling that to have someone pull on a thread of your underlying logic and watch it unravel, even if your team was confident in the proposed solution. The impressions made in those moments will definitely color the confidence a company has in allowing you to continue your pursuit, especially through the ambiguity inherent in pursuing innovation. Contributing our design work is table stakes, but we must also have our *why* codified into guiding principles for design too. This is not to say that we need to present our design arguments with 100 percent completeness and perfection. These arguments could be low-fi in divergence and hi-fi in convergence. However, your guiding principles for design can help get the room comfortable with 80 percent of the rhyme and reason behind your ideas and assure everyone that the team is working from a credible foundation before they can think of asking the first question. They'll be more inclined to help you then, rather than question you.

Also, in a world where the digital paradigms feed a never-ending cycle of marketers marketing and consumers consuming, we can use guiding principles for design to illuminate where we want to intentionally veer from this unsustainable paradigm and break the boundaries of convention to explore more of the downstream implications of our work. Whether it's the future of AI (navigating trust, data privacy, or intellectual property rights) or having a team problem-solve ideas to ensure that a new business model contributes to social good, guiding principles for design can shine a light on key convictions important to the team and your most important stakeholders and target audiences. As you explain your next round of wireframes, user flows, industrial design sketches, or data visualizations, your guiding principles for design can highlight where the team will make a stand on data ethics, sustainability, responsible practices, social outreach, antiracist positions, decolonization, equity-centered problem-solving, and the like. I'm tremendously inspired by pioneers such as Chris Rudd or Dori Tunstall, PhD, who wire their business platforms and practices with these convictions at the very forefront of their problem-solving approach. Unfortunately, the amount of time most enterprises spend on these topics is still miniscule. Force their hand. Widen their aperture to include these considerations in your problem-solving because your stakeholders care and probably want to know what you're doing about them. These considerations will likely intersect with any product or service you intend to sell.

## MULTIDISCIPLINARY FEEDBACK

We've previously highlighted the challenges that multidisciplinary teams face in building up their chemistry to collaborate effectively, but it can get rather tricky when it comes time to soliciting feedback from the same team. For feedback-specific meetings, we typically also invite a broader set of stakeholders (executive sponsors, outside advisors, external subject matter experts [SMEs], etc.), who could each bring very different mindsets and perspectives to the conversation. They might not have been exposed to the full journey made by your existing team, and their input can seem very cold and jarring without appropriate efforts to acclimate them to the context of where things are as of the time of the meeting. Where do we even begin? Each participant in a feedback meeting may have different drivers for what they deem to be important. From my experience, I believe it is absolutely critical to proactively facilitate each feedback conversation to ensure the time together is as valuable as it can be. A feedback session will be deemed successful when all team members feel like they have new perspectives and insights from the feedback that will help inform the next steps or key decisions concretely. Because of the different disciplines informing these conversations, we should remember a few techniques in the backs of our minds to steer the conversation effectively depending on where we are in the process.

As we've characterized the process as a nonlinear journey through the forest of ambiguity, there may be times in the process where the team is diverging and creating a lot of ideas. Hopefully, you'll have a large number of early concepts to share when you're ready for feedback against divergent thinking. To facilitate this scenario, it may make sense to arrange early ideas into a gallery or exhibit of sorts. This can be done in person in a large team room or virtually using a whiteboarding platform like Miro (formerly RealtimeBoard).[2] You can arrange the meeting agenda to give people time to peruse the room's walls of early concepts and vote on their favorites. After a while, you can convene the team together to discuss which concepts garnered the most votes or interest as well as concepts that were perhaps interesting outliers away from the clusters of common affinity. As the conversation focuses on a select few, you could break up the larger group into smaller groups to add richer fidelity to the feedback. For each of those most interesting concepts, what did the groups like about them? What would they change? How would they extend or stretch them? What additional questions did the concepts evoke? What additional ideas or outside inspirations (i.e., exemplars) did the concept spark from memory? Garnering this type of feedback will help sustain and increase the momentum for more divergent ideation, giving your teams confidence that they'll eventually find even better ideas using the feedback as fuel for your momentum.

During the throes of convergence, we should expect each design proposal to speak as a cohesive concept that can hold water with each multidisciplinary stakeholder, no matter if the solutioning is incremental to the business, a new, greenfield venture, or blue-sky exploration. Aside from pinning up the relevant design assets (wireframes, sketches, etc.) and their corresponding guiding principles for design, the solutioning should be arranged to speak to the basic elements of how it will help the business meet or exceed certain objectives (i.e., an elevator pitch, more or less, with a clear potential return on investment) such that a sponsor might consider investing funds or resources to move it forward. For any converged concept, we'd expect to find the following elements in its presentation:

- *Name of the solution:* This could be a temporary, pithy nickname that describes the *what* very simply. This name doesn't have to be permanent; you might introduce or revisit a brand strategy surrounding the opportunity if the concept merits further work downstream.
- *Mission statement:* This should speak quickly to its intended purpose.
- *Customers and stakeholders:* Who is the solution intending to serve?
- *Problem:* What is the problem or friction being addressed?
- *Solution:* What is the value proposition being offered; visualized by wireframes, sketches, functional prototypes, infographics, and so on; and rationalized with key guiding principles for design presented in parallel?
- *Features:* What are the key winning features of this idea?
- *Impact:* What are the expected market implications of introducing this solution? In early convergence, this might be a back-of-the-envelope rough estimate.

Once we have these elements, a multidisciplinary audience will gain an initial sense of the holistic rationale of each concept, helping them focus where they can offer helpful feedback versus rehashing fundamental ground just to understand the concept's underlying rationale. Let's do what we can to present in a way that feels complete to the multidisciplinary opportunity in order to avoid wasting time.

Assuming we do a good job fully characterizing our solutions, we are ready to pitch our concepts to our multidisciplinary team and broader stakeholders, and then open the floor up for effective feedback. To facilitate such a session, you might set an agenda where you allow the team the opportunity to pitch each concept, followed by an equal share of discussion time with the audience. At BCGDV, we used a number of easy digital tools to give each stakeholder the ability to rate the quality of the concept against a sliding scale, individually. The meeting facilitator could quickly assess which convergent concepts were getting the most attention and facilitate a larger group conversation with that survey data in hand. For concepts that were the most interesting, we could then have concerted discussions along the following four dimensions:

1. *Desirability:* Does this solution actually matter to someone? Do we have the correct set of representative stakeholders characterized? Is anyone missing? Do we have their value criteria clearly synthesized? Have we shared the concept with them and gotten any feedback? Is there a moment of truth to be had from this concept?

2. *Business viability:* Can we actually create value for the business with this solution, whether it's monetary, information, or social value? Can we assert a strategic advantage with this solution in relation to our competition? Does this solution actually yield profitable, sustainable, and responsible growth? What business risks does this solution create?

3. *Technical feasibility:* Will this solution work? Can we get it done using our technical capabilities and within the roadmap that we've forecasted? How easy is it, how hard is it, or how manageable is it with respect to competing priorities? Do we have the right experts on the team to get this done? Can we connect to capabilities outside our team?

4. *Strategic alignment:* Is this solution right for our company to take on? Does it fit our company mission and values? Do we have the right array of capabilities to make this solution happen? Should we build it ourselves or partner with the right capabilities in an open-source manner? Is there a start-up already doing this that we might acquire?

Facilitating concerted discussions along these four dimensions is surely going to give the team the right feedback to inform the next steps. With full humility in mind, an outcome might be to halt a concept: "Let's not invest any more time because the feedback says we're off track or the impact isn't significant enough to warrant further effort." Otherwise, hopefully the feedback we collect provides signals on how we can improve the levels of desirability, viability, feasibility, and strategic alignment for each convergent design proposal that is still on the table.

## CHAPTER 7

## YOUR BANDWIDTH

It seems that everyone is busier and busier these days. Even with the advent of hybrid or remote working, the lines between our professional and personal lives continue to blur. We're always "on," and we're still wrestling with the good and bad of all of it. When we think about how we work, I've found it helpful to always take a step back and inventory the different categories of activity where I tend to spend time. Some sage mentors in my journey have nudged me to always evaluate the short- and long-term context of the things in which I engage. Where do they fall on the rubric of urgent versus important? As strategy spans to include the voices of more disciplines, the number of stakeholders we need to serve will only increase based on the complexity of our challenges and opportunities. Thus, we can assume that the demand on our time is sure to increase. In my last few roles (especially helping to stand up newly formed multidisciplinary teams), my calendar was often double- and triple-booked within those efforts. I could rarely walk the hallways without being pinged or interrupted by someone's needs. While I'm happy to serve as best I can, I realized I couldn't fulfill every request, much less fulfill them with quality and enough sincerity. I also noticed that far too many things were claiming to be urgent but were not necessarily important to our team's critical milestones or the company's long-term objectives.

While navigating BCG, I benefited from a particular leadership training course that sought to illuminate my stress triggers and how they related to how I managed my time and prioritized my responsibilities. With the insights gleaned, I started to look at my calendar very differently. Looking ahead at short-, mid-, and long-term milestones, I blocked my calendar to ensure the important work was being addressed with a concerted investment in focus time. While an initial improvement, I had to probe even further to eliminate any unnecessary friction that prevented me from bringing my best self to work. As I reflected on my usual day-to-day and week-to-week rhythm, I noticed I could categorize my activities into the following three areas:

• *Stakeholder management:* Keeping client executive stakeholders and sponsors up to speed and strategically aligned to our plan, the resources required, and the approaches used to execute the plan. Communication needs might be required on a daily, weekly, monthly, or quarterly basis.

• *Communication production:* Creating documentation, presentation materials, and design deliverables that codify preceding problem-solving activities for the purposes of fulfilling stakeholder communications. This is the time spent actually documenting, even though some folks may use this activity as a medium to problem-solve as they create deliverables.

• *Creative problem-solving:* Engaging in the deep work to make critical sparks and connections between disparate inputs, data points, inspirations, and relevant trends to creatively conceive, shape, or structure new solutions that meaningfully solve a latent need or friction. This usually requires a nonlinear journey of discovery, divergent ideation, convergent ideation, and any pivots toward a relevant, intuitive solution.

As a designer, the third category is arguably the most important for what I bring to the table, which informs the substance that will go into making the first two categories more successful if we're intentional about the balance across them.

I will be even bolder and say that the third category is constantly under threat in the hustle and bustle of the business world. Executive stakeholders want their status updates and want to feel connected to the work even with their limited mindshare available to invest in any one single project among the many initiatives on their roadmap. During my time at BCGDV, we did our best to cultivate a different dynamic. Our different venture teams actually hosted client team members as an integral part of each venture team. This was a new and novel approach compared to typical management consulting, and rightly so because our charter was different: to innovate and incubate new businesses. In classic management consulting, a firm prides itself on its ability to sustain thoughtful, intimate, and high-impact client relationships, always showing value at every step as a part of the commercial relationship. Consulting firms send their folks to their client locations to spend as much time as possible providing high-value problem-solving across a wide range of business topics. BCGDV represented a very unique corporate venturing platform focused on innovation and business build. Client embeds were asked to live in residence with us at our strategically placed innovation centers all around the world. For each member of a venture team, we had to foster an inclusive dynamic of team collaboration regardless of who might be signing a teammate's paycheck. We fostered the idea of "one team," and every venture had to create a flat team atmosphere to function like a lean start-up in which everyone could find an amenable balance for how they spent their bandwidth.

## OPEN APERTURE

We must prioritize time to see beyond our immediate day-to-day realities and circumstances. Look up. Look out. Look beyond the walls of your team room. It's very important. I'm often asked, "How does one stay creative as a designer, businessperson, or technologist?" I believe it requires maintaining an open aperture ahead of or in the midst of any opportunity you are problem-solving for. While we need to be thoughtful to ensure we're delivering on our organization's near-term objectives, we always need to have our eyes also scanning the expansive horizon and have faith that we'll always discover something new, useful, and inspiring to expand or enrich our point of view. If we remember the future foresight lens from figure 1.4, we can always scan to identify people we might serve one day even though our business may not prioritize them right now. We can study emerging paradigms within industries that are challenging previously held assumptions and question what that can mean for us within our own organization. We can keep track of interesting trends that have potential to inspire the art of what's possible and how these trends might color future scenarios. We should consider the full range of trend categories spanning social, technological, economic, environmental, policy, and energy-related movements that are affecting every industry. Finally, we can identify the exemplars (i.e., the living proof of those trends taking shape) by earmarking the luminaries, start-ups, research institutions, and enterprises doing interesting work that might inspire our thinking.

We can even cultivate an open aperture within our own individual career journeys. How do you do that? If anything, try to stay immersed in streams of never-ending inspiration. I make a little bit of time for it every day. It could be as easy as picking up my smartphone and tapping into the social media streams and posts from luminaries I greatly respect. For example, following John Maeda's work (before even meeting him) introduced me to the likes of Kat Holmes; Natalie Nixon, PhD; Jessica Helfand; and organizations like the MIT Media Lab. His feed gave me interesting tentacles of inspiration to follow through on and investigate. Similarly, every week, I try to dive into a different book in an area of curiosity or relating to the work I'm engaged in for my client partners. Every month, I try to get out of the house and purposely go see something inspirational. In Los Angeles, we have a plethora of museums, art galleries, interesting bookstores, and cultural venues like Japan House in Los Angeles (see figure 7.3), with an always rotating series of cultural exhibitions.[3] Finally, my house and home office are chock-full of inspirations from all of these investigations. If I have a moment of boredom, I can pick up a book or a design artifact and set my creative mind in motion again. Enrich your individual trajectory by making time to invest in your own curiosity. Ensure your work environment instigates curiosity as well.

Having an open aperture is critical for teams and organizations too. I believe it's possible to cultivate open-source connections

**Figure 7.3**
Visiting Japan House in Los Angeles, California, with my son to engage in some fun spatial, interactive activities that mix culture and technology.

with people and communities outside your immediate business concerns that you might leverage downstream in your projects. When observing BCG consultants, I noticed that many of them were constantly writing or giving talks on the learnings that came from their day-to-day case work. With BCG being a very intellectually curious culture, I grew to understand how important it was that they stay connected to outside industry-focused communities. The speaking and writing opportunities weren't about ego stroking. As I started to follow suit in putting myself out there to write and speak about my unique design experiences, I noticed that the more I shared, the more I freed my mind up to learn from others within communities that existed outside my day-to-day work. I brought back new insights, best practices, and external relationships that greatly benefited my teams. We hired some of those folks we met. You have to pick the right communities that align with the ambitions you have internally. As we were scaling design capabilities inside BCGDV, my team was leaning heavily on the DMI to exchange inspirations and best practices that allowed us to keep our aperture wide through all the paces of our growth.[4]

Conversely, the risk of not investing in maintaining your open aperture for curiosity, creativity, and future foresight is navigating forward with a myopic set of blind spots. Your attention, mindset, and conscious and subconscious behaviors will become hardened within the language of your existing realities and business circumstances. You'll find you'll keep rehashing the same old insights, data points, and perspectives that got the business to where it is today but will not get you to where your business needs to go based on newly emerging paradigms. You or your organization might already be putting limiters on your platform's potential because maybe you only have executed one type of product in your history, but newly emerging realities are pointing to new needs that require a different set of intuitive offerings that could be yours to pursue. If you're with an athletics brand that's historically made athletic apparel and sneakers, you might not realize you have an opportunity to create an offense around connected home exercise equipment or wearables on the go. I am amazed at the quick-strike penetration of start-up brands like Tonal, Peloton, and lululemon Studio (formerly Mirror), compared to incumbent brands that have dominated the athletics space for decades. Leveraging design at parity and maintaining an open aperture can inspire future possibilities for your organization, even if those capabilities aren't quite available for you yet. They could be if you have an open aperture and the balance of patience and proactiveness to strike when the right variables fall into place.

## DIVERSITY, EQUITY, AND INCLUSION

The inclination to open your and your team's aperture depends significantly on who is in the room. I'm speaking beyond the formality of titles and professional disciplines. I want to focus on the people when it comes to DEI. While teams need to be more multidisciplinary to match the complexity of our needs now and into the future, it's also important to ensure that the room is full of folks that represent the cultures, dreams, mindsets, lived experiences, and needs of the demographics we serve. As the world becomes smaller thanks to digital connectivity, our global society will only become more and more diverse. Our multidisciplinary teams should strive to mirror the diverse tapestry that is the world across gender, race, background, intersectionalities, lived experience, and so on. This will help us more seamlessly collaborate with our audiences because we actually *are* them, not just designing *for* them from an ivory tower position. Unfortunately, when we interrogate the makeup of most design and innovation organizations, the teams we see do not mirror those audiences they claim to serve. This leads to a lot of the mismatches and myopic business precedents we continue to experience in the market. Not only is it a moral imperative to do the right thing in serving a diverse society, but we also leave a considerable amount of business on the table by not serving society with relevant products and services that are in tune with their mindsets and sensibilities.

Now, at the same time, I can only speak to my personal and professional lived experience. I am a Black man who's navigated very unique multidisciplinary leaps through corporate America. Through those transitions across engineering, business, and design, I experienced a lot of resistance beyond any constructive critique of the work itself. I and my identity were under critique: "You don't belong here." When forced to guess the motivations for such pushback, I assumed an unfortunate tax when spending time and energy trying to understand that or the effort required to navigate around the resistance. All that is to say that I know what it feels like to be marginalized: the body language of unacceptance, the unfounded gossip questioning my pedigree or simply not acknowledging my contributions while endorsing mediocrity from others. This is the covert assault that too many marginalized people have to deal with. The elders in my family had it far worse, and their stories broach the overt category of assault. When I look at the field of design, I am appalled that Black representation sits at roughly 3 percent, and perhaps lower depending on the specific design specialty.[5] Contrast that with the population in the United States, representing roughly 13 percent Black folks, and even much higher percentages in key markets, where it can be as high as 50 percent. For brands, companies, and agencies, are we to believe that Black folks are not worthy? Do we not have merit to belong? Many companies use Black folks as consumers and sources of culture, but I don't see them hiring us—at least, not nearly enough. It's even worse when looking at their executive teams and boardrooms. It shouldn't be this way, but we have to be honest about what we see. The needle has barely moved.

At the same time, I have had a fair share of privilege and know what that feels like too. As a male navigating some of these professional spaces, I am often given the benefit of the doubt compared to my colleagues of a different gender. Several years ago, I was part of a large workshop leading a group through an important brainstorming activity. I couldn't help but notice the one Black woman in the room, and I noticed her hand was trembling under the table. She voiced some of the most profound and insightful contributions, but she was clearly rehearsing what she had to say before she could say it in a room where white men were the majority. That image of her hand trembling is seared into my memory. I can't pretend to know what it's like for Black women who might be experiencing double the resistance based on race and gender. I can't speak to someone else's lived experience. It's more meaningful for people with these lived experiences to have their say themselves. I should be learning from them when they do it and say, "thank you." They should feel encouraged to bring their full selves to whatever space they inhabit and feel a sense of belonging, and know that their unique gifts, potential, and skill sets matter in the room. If there's anything I can do, it is to be a role model for the right servant-leadership behaviors to create that sense of belonging for any team under my care. Unfortunately, we have to navigate a world where some are comfortable relishing in their power and privileges while others suffer marginalization. There are some that believe in the myth of meritocracy and do not believe that societal imbalance plays a role in where they are in life, or where they sit in the workplace.

Even after a season of heightened social awareness, in as much as it took watching Black bodies dying in the streets at the hands of police brutality or AAPI (Asian American and Pacific Islander) hate crimes spawning from the COVID-19 pandemic, the pendulum of concern is already shifting to an opposite and unfortunate place. You no longer hear as much messaging or as many social media posts coming from enterprises in addressing these paradigms. When employees in 2020 felt like they could openly share their worries, concerns, and fears with their coworkers, they were reminded to keep their attention on the company objectives and leave the social ills at home. Corporate America has grown tired of talking about DEI, and any discussion of social inequity is couched under the guise of being "woke," political, or divisive. This has been further stoked by far-right-leaning figures in tech, media, and business. Founders from the likes of Coinbase and Basecamp have made their positions quite clear. I'll paraphrase their announcements: "leave your social issues and activism at the door." Or maybe you can glean insight from their blog posts, like "The Waning Days of DEI's Dominance."[6] I don't have to show you what Elon Musk's anti-woke leanings have done to the platform formerly known as Twitter. That is the unfortunate climate right now as I write this book. My father warned me and my siblings about the pendulum of concern (or lack thereof) swinging back and forth. My father, Lonnie Bethune, presently serves as the chief operating officer for my company.

In my father's long career, he ascended the ladder to general retail management roles (including a lot of HR experience), doing all the right things, functioning as a high performer and usually one of the only BIPOC leaders in any role he was assigned. Because he was considered a positive role model, he was pulled into DEI work to help thousands of other employees understand what DEI could mean for their local territories, in terms of business advantage and merchandising relevance. He was among four high-potential employees who were eventually certified as DEI facilitators and assigned to bring their respective US regions up to speed through a series of traveling workshops. To be clear, the intended audiences were primarily white and male. The facilitators encountered immediate opposition, with many attendees feeling like it was a waste of time to discuss social issues, nor did they care to prioritize advancement for BIPOC and women peers. If anything, the sessions revealed (1) that DEI and affirmative action programs were considered threats to existing power structures, and (2) that that same majority would follow an unwritten rule to self-protect their interests by mobilizing as a group to resist, confirming my father's fears and doubts about the underbelly of corporate America. BIPOC employees were challenged aggressively following those sessions. This resulted in many being put on undesirable assignments, receiving poorer ratings, and eventually being forced to resign or face termination. White women fared better in their careers from the DEI work, but it was disastrously worse for BIPOC women facing the most severe scrutiny. The more the DEI work advanced, the further behind my father saw BIPOC associates across the management ranks.

When I reflect on what my father had to deal with as a Black man in corporate America, I seethe in anger. He graciously offers his children insight into his lived experiences so that we can have a better shot at success. It should be "easier" for future generations, but I'm not so sure it is. At the same time, I still believe there is innate goodness in people, and most people want to do the right thing. Despite overcoming their adversities, my parents taught us children to see the good in folks. I believe they far outnumber the bad folks who hold onto fear, ignorance, and hate. If we share that core human imperative to uplift one another in the pursuit of DEI, then we have to rally together as a community and be bolder with our actions. Beyond that moral imperative, let's recognize that it also hurts our business concerns to not support DEI. Otherwise, our blind spots will continue to be a problem and we will become quickly irrelevant to a hyperconnected, diverse world that cares about celebrating differences and inclusion. As enterprise leaders continue to vacillate on their level of commitment to DEI, they may not realize they are already woefully late to the party as their audiences are already moving quickly beyond them. Conversely, by investing in DEI and empowering your employees to bring their full selves to work, you will stay connected to culture, maintain relevance, and be better equipped to handle uncertainty. Choose to be late to the party, or choose to be in the know when you have folks that authentically match the societies you claim to serve.

In the pursuit of innovation, there are no guarantees of inevitable success. It's a mixture of being proactive while also appreciating the role that uncertainty and serendipity have in creating the conditions for lightning to strike. Ideally, the result is something new and novel and hopefully meaningful for your most important stakeholders. Taking each step in the forest of ambiguity is less about definitive right and wrong, and more about establishing momentum to make the best choices based on the information you have at each step. Much like a flywheel helps a motor maintain steady performance or Collins's characterization of small wins that put company growth on cruise control, I hope these accelerants give you a sense of how they can increase your odds of catching lightning in a bottle. Without them, you may be more vulnerable to headwinds. Whether it's using guiding principles for design to bring people along, managing your bandwidth, cultivating the right types of feedback, or deeply committing to DEI, successfully innovating largely depends on the people you have that are working hard to serve your stakeholders. I'm reminded of my friend Mauro Porcini, chief design officer of PepsiCo, and his wonderful book, *The Human Side of Innovation: The Power of People in Love with People.*[7] "We are entering the age of excellence, a new world in which every company will always have a greater need for design-driven innovation—an entirely humanist type of innovation with a sincere, obsessive, unavoidable attention to the needs and wants of every human being." Porcini's words give me hope that the business world will and should turn a better corner.

• • •

### Takeaways: Finding Accelerants to Our Aims

• Elevate guiding principles for design that fully explain the *why* behind your design and product iterations and subsequent decisions. When soliciting feedback, embrace an additive mindset through divergence and a discerning venture mindset through convergence of your ideas.

• Be mindful of the activities that consume your time from day to day and week to week. If you want to participate in creative problem-solving, recognize how your time allocations actually reveal how much you're able to do that compared to stakeholder management and routine production work.

• Open your aperture and always scan the future time horizon for new inspiration to inform the work you're doing today. At the same time, recognize the myopic blind spots of your organization, and evolve your team's makeup to mirror the world through investments in DEI.

## 8 FINAL THOUGHTS

EMBRACE YOUR NONLINEARITY.

I think it's fair to say that the world is in turmoil. Recently, we've witnessed invasions, a global pandemic (still lingering with new COVID-19 variants), xenophobia, racism, political divisiveness, antisemitism, terrorism, islamophobia, genocides, a loneliness epidemic, growing economic disparities, and the ongoing threat of climate change. It's easy to feel discouraged with so many variables feeling out of our control. But deep down, each of us knows that we have unique gifts placed within us that can help change the course of events. History has shown that we are capable of bringing forward our ingenuity, resilience, creativity, and courage to confront any adversity. The last few years have forced us to question previously held assumptions like never before. With our unprecedented connectivity, our society can connect the dots, visualize problems, and ask harder questions to inform activism, social movements, and new innovations. Connectivity also leaves us vulnerable to potential disinformation that is spread by nefarious actors. By sheer effect, dimensions of trust, providence, and credibility will be highly valued commodities as we move forward. While we may not have immediate solutions to our challenges, we can have faith that embarking on a journey of exploration will lead us somewhere meaningful. In a seemingly dark world, we need more lights to guide our path. As you're reading this book, I hope you see yourself as a light who's capable of leading by example.

Granted, I write this while attempting to crack the glass ceiling of ambiguity regarding design's place within the realm of business and multidisciplinary collaboration. Innovation, guided by design, can serve as a catalyst for change. We can innovate to show up for people differently. We can innovate to improve how we show up for each other. We can innovate to radically change how we show up for our planet. While these are noble ambitions, how can we think about the many ways to go about it? I find it's a juxtaposition between setting bold, visionary aspirations and recognizing our present realities. Because most of us have to devote the entirety of our day toward making a living, we tend to think about innovation largely through the lens of the workplace. The workplace may include start-ups, enterprises, institutions, governments, and NGOs. These entities represent the launching pads where we can manifest our ideas. At the same time, we offer so much more than our job titles and rote job descriptions. Each of us bring lived experiences, values, and deep-seeded convictions into and through these spaces. At the same time, our nature may run at odds with the hardened paths previously forged from industrialization, capitalism, politics, and traditional patriarchal structures. But we don't have to accept the status quo. If we remember our own humanity and connect with the humanity of our target audiences, we'll see the gaps, mismatches, and biases more clearly. We'll develop an intrinsic motivation to do something about it. We'll want to innovate.

But do we have permission or agency to innovate from our current positions in the workplace? Do we have the mandate to innovate? I remember wrestling with innovation topics with my first employer, Westinghouse Electric Company, a leading original equipment manufacturer (OEM) within the nuclear power industry. Our mandate to innovate actually permeated the very core of the business. Within existing product lines and service offerings, no engineering project ever mapped to formulaic convention. We constantly had to innovate out of necessity because there were always too many surprises to thwart any predictability. We always had to make tweaks and adapt on the fly. I learned to "inspect what you don't expect" from one of my first managers, Dan Trombola, who led Westinghouse's reactor mechanical systems group at the time. We had to anticipate surprises and think quickly on our feet to derive solutions while inhibiting any adverse impact to a plant's critical-path schedule. In parallel with our efforts to support the core business, we had the license to propose innovation projects. Any employee could make suggestions via an online portal, and if your idea had merit, you could pitch your concept to a panel of engineering leaders, and they could grant you a budget and people to advance your idea. I absolutely loved that experience. It allowed me to coauthor a new product line in the process and earn my first US utility patent as a young engineer.

I worked for another organization with a clearer delineation between the core business and its innovation capabilities. However, it lacked a portal or pitching mechanism for employees to freely submit their proposals. Employees could use their relationships to socialize ideas, but there was no guarantee they would be heard. Because of my brewing convictions for multidisciplinary work, I wanted to work in their innovation groups. However, some chose not to "see" me playing in that arena. Innovation was for a privileged few, and you needed special authorization to access their department. I persisted and literally showed the organization I was capable of contributing through stretch assignments. They acknowledged my contributions but saw me as a foreign entity compared to that which was familiar to them: "Your career didn't start here. If it's between you and someone who started here ten to fifteen years ago, we're picking that person every single time." My prior experiences didn't matter, and that was made very clear: "The work we do here is hard." I did nothing short of acknowledging that from the very beginning, but you know what? Cutting my teeth on reactors was hard too. When it came down to brass tacks skills and concrete success criteria, their feedback was not very clear as to why I couldn't play. Their resistance was very subjective, typical of gatekeeping behavior. Swallowing my disappointment, I had to learn to pick up my ball and find another place to play. Thankfully, I learned how to take ownership of my career and eventually found a plethora of opportunities to innovate and serve multidisciplinary innovation teams.

When I do reflect back on my early work experiences, I may have perceived innovation perhaps through too narrow of a lens. For right, wrong, or indifferent, I thought it meant entertaining "what's next," building on previous generations of product to introduce the next incremental advancement. It meant conceiving the next-gen automobile, the next high-tech sneaker, or the next smartphone. But as we understand the perils of hyperconsumption, we're now questioning what it is that we actually need. Instead of leasing or buying a car, how can we think about mobility very differently and through a wider aperture of possibilities? How do we innovate for the underlying needs of going from one location to another versus pushing another car for sale? Ultimately, we need to question how we show up for people. How are we innovating to unlock human potential? How are we actually fostering human connection? How are we innovating to address loneliness? How are we inspiring a path toward meaning and happiness? How are we making our efforts mean more than just merely marketers marketing and consumers consuming? How can we make a difference and still make sure everyone is made whole in terms of valuing their time, resources, and expertise? I'm not against making money per se, but I'm all for exploring a more humane, respectful, and restorative approach to bringing meaningful innovations into the world to make our lives and the planet better.

With today's climate of economic uncertainty, innovation as a capability can easily find itself under threat, as well as the people responsible for informing it. In times of budget scrutiny, an organization's focus may shift completely toward the needs of the core business and what it deems as the most critical set of capabilities.

Per our previous observations of precedent, the business world might not value the creative capabilities that could inform innovation. Design, being the least understood discipline at the problem-solving table, is especially vulnerable. If we only view design's value as worth the final 1 to 5 percent of any value chain or the final aesthetic overlay, then we might deprioritize it when money and bandwidth become tight. Unfortunately, we've recently witnessed a large swath of layoffs disproportionately affecting design across several industries. Wall Street tends to further instigate this dilemma when they see one company cutting costs and begin asking when the next company will follow suit. A company bringing on a new CEO with a mandate for operational efficiency can exacerbate this tendency. Creative disciplines such as design or marketing may be the first to get slashed as companies get ahead of potential headwinds. Some highly regarded design and innovation shops like IDEO were not immune to having to let their people go either.[1] It makes me wonder if these paradigms cause some companies to unknowingly shoot themselves in the foot. By reacting in the short term, they are cutting off the people that could inform a sustaining innovation pipeline that would keep their company relevant now and into the future.

Even with these challenges, fortune will favor the brave if we do two things. First, we must lean into our curiosity despite the adversities and headwinds that creep up. If we think about the audiences we serve and the key stakeholders that orbit them, there are latent needs waiting to be uncovered and solved. Even when the economy stagnates or old precedents creep back into the picture, you need to still lean in and connect the dots between needs and ideas. Even when the mandate to "innovate" slips off the rails, you can still lean in and use your curiosity. What that does is kick off a domino effect regardless of the circumstances. Curiosity begets experimentation, which opens the door for creativity to come in and inform what we can accomplish. Experimentation begets evidence, which we can hold up to build our confidence and credibility that we're heading in the right direction. Second, we must allow that evidence to shape our convictions. Once we have some time to digest patterns from many cycles of investigation, ideation, and testing, the evidence we garner will surely speak to us (and others). It will resonate with us because our full humanity will hear it, see it, and consider it deeply within our conscious, a conscious heavily informed by the full weight of our lived experiences. Your convictions will compel you to move forward to do something to address those gaps that speak ill to your core beliefs and values.

While I'm conscious that the degree of agency, permission, or bandwidth to innovate may vary for each of us and our teams, I believe we can always use our curiosity and convictions to instigate opportunities to create something new. Call it *sheer will*. Even if we're not allowed to call it *innovation*, that is surely what we'll cultivate if we keep seeking to learn and if we keep making things to meet the needs we find. We'll bring ourselves and our teams to the entrance of the forest of ambiguity in pursuit of innovation (see figure 8.1). Some circles might call this the "fuzzy front end" of any innovation or product development journey. Heading straight forward in a formulaic way might have you crashing into a tree unable to make sense of things through the fog. Instead, let's further contextualize the ground that we've covered by thinking about the preceding chapters with a slight twist of nonlinearity.

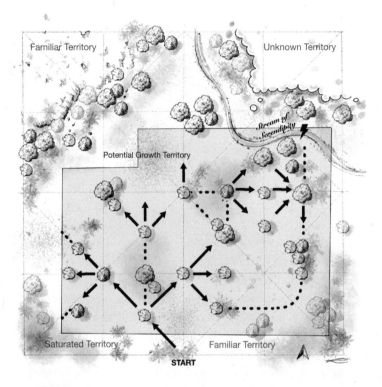

**Figure 8.1**
The innovation journey is full of guideposts where we intuitively make
the best choice based on the best information we have at each moment.

## QUAL IS THE CLAY, QUANT IS THE FRAME

In our efforts to satiate our curiosity, we'll come across research findings and takeaways in every shape and variety. Roughly speaking, we can categorize all learnings we have as either qualitative (*qual*) or quantitative (*quant*) in nature. Quant usually contains conclusive data that states facts about segmentation, market size, discretionary spend, market share, financial performance, and operational efficiency expressed as key performance indicators (KPIs). It's matter of fact, and that's helpful for us to make data-driven decisions on where to spend our time with always limited resources. As we think about innovation in the context of business, quant helps us frame boundary conditions and inform vectors of exploration that will help the company grow and remain relevant with its audiences. However, while helpful for strategic planning and prioritization, the nature of quant is rather shallow. It lacks the depth of substance that we need to begin shaping solutions against the needs and opportunities we're trying to address. We have to find the substance that qual can give us through different vectors of design investigative inquiry. We're going to have to commit more time to find the substance, or "clay," and it will be a nonlinear and nuanced dance to find it. But it's important that we find it so that we can shape useful, relevant, and emotionally resonance experiences.

For this clay to make an impact downstream and influence the broader multidisciplinary team, we have put thoughtful effort into carefully synthesizing key insights and opportunities. We want to avoid presenting a bunch of consensuses to our leadership teams about things we already know (a "snooze fest"). That will hurt our credibility and any future research efforts may be viewed with scrutiny. We need to bubble up the top critical insights that will get people really excited to come up with new solutions against a latent need or critical friction in our stakeholders' experience. The innovation logic that spawns from each insight needs to be solid. Per Katherine Bennett's counsel, "An insight leads to an opportunity. Ideation leads to an idea. That's an unbreakable chain," and something to continually reinforce.[2] Otherwise, we might lose our stakeholders in bringing them along our chosen vectors. Like a miner panning for gold, we have to put in considerable work to scan, affinity-map, sort, and codify the takeaways across our workshop outputs, one-on-one interview notes, video footage, photo observations, and transcripts. Then, we need to translate our findings into effective syntheses and visual tools to help our team make decisions and feel like they can make focused contributions based on a clear understanding of customer wants and needs. Our syntheses may include representative personas, stakeholder journeys, or system maps that clearly distill the value criteria and the exchanges of value that are most important through our stakeholders' and customers' experiences.

### DIVERGE, CONVERGE, PIVOT, AND DIVERGE AGAIN

Design plays a critical role in creating the future. Personally, I love every opportunity to conceive something new against an unmet need. While design plays a leading voice in the creative journey, design should not go about it alone. The multidisciplinary team should be brought along. Everyone should have equal opportunity to inform ideas and contribute their expertise, so long as they respect each discipline's voice around the table at parity. Design can become a "team sport" in this respect. But teaming will require a unique tactic of orchestrating the different voices, problem-solving styles, and pools of deep expertise that are available around the table. We need to know when to collaborate and when to afford individual breathing room. We should embrace the businessperson leveraging hypothesis-first and deductive thinking styles against the findings we have, the technologist leveraging inductive thinking and experimentation, and the designer who's leveraging more abductive, bottom-up reasoning to sense-make our opportunities. It will feel awkward at first, but the team will learn to see creative sparks and connections from their differences. They'll have more ingredients to conceive ideas than when they started. We must have a mindset to *fall forward* (nodding to Denzel Washington's commencement talk at the University of Pennsylvania). We need to be fluid, try things, and embrace failure as a necessity and make our teams feel safe doing so.

In casting the net of ideas wide, we find that exercising divergent ideation takes discipline. If we have a mindset to diverge from the start of every ideation opportunity, then we avoid the tendency to jump to one solution based on our hunches or team consensus. That one hypothesis might be absolutely right in the end, but we're never setting ourselves back by imagining alternative and multiple solution ideas for an uncovered need. Let's ensure we're empowering individuals to come up with as many ideas as they'd like without premature judgment. When we're together as a group, we should embrace a mindset of "yes, and," no matter if we're mind-mapping, brainstorming, sketching thumbnail iterations, or picking different areas along the stakeholder journey to generate more ideas. As we continue to diverge, design can play a hand in helping the multidisciplinary team craft early concepts, stories, and system sketches in order to help visualize compelling divergent concepts for broader team and stakeholder consideration. The designer in the room will instinctively know how to use visuals to produce compelling, yet lo-fi expressions of each idea. It's about falling forward with the swiftness of the Sharpie. When a designer is paired with another discipline and its different thinking style, divergent thinking can really accelerate as teammates marry their complementary thoughts together.

When we feel we have enough ideas on the table, it's time to turn that corner toward convergence, weaving together elements from the best thinking into integrated solutions that pass our different lenses of discernment (remember desirability, viability, feasibility, and strategic alignment). Will each solution proposal really matter to the stakeholders we're targeting? Will each proposal speak to the business viability, financial upside, and competitive advantage? Will each solution be feasible to build? Can we even do it with our present technical capabilities, or do we need to partner with someone in our market landscape? How easy or hard will it be? What is the expected impact with our target audience and the resulting market implication in terms of the size of the business opportunity? At both an individual and team level, a multidisciplinary team must wrestle with answering these questions as they iterate and pitch the solution to their critical stakeholders and sponsors. These questions surely are not easy to answer, and certain ideas (we'll inevitably learn) will just not work out. We should have the discipline to "call it," to dismantle the thinking and pivot toward a new vector. We might need to seek more information, resynthesize better insights, and diverge again. Even within a converged solution, there may need to be a section of it that we need to reconsider and we may need to exercise divergence to flush out a better option among many alternative options. Effective learning warrants that we stop, pivot, regroup, diverge, converge, and diverge again. This is the reality of the innovation journey, and we should embrace its nonlinearity.

## BREAK FORMULAIC CONVENTION

For any innovation endeavor that I have the privilege of being a part of, I always ask the following question: "How are we showing up meaningfully for people when and where they need us the most, and on their terms?" What could be potential moments of truth in their lives? That's my first concern over simply ushering someone through a company's marketing funnel. If we take care of these questions with intention, the funnel, its metrics, and the overarching business will be fine. I worry about the ever-accelerating paradigm of marketers marketing, consumers consuming. It's unsustainable and fails to interrogate how to meet people where they are in their journey. For any digital experience, it feels like we're always being ushered to "click to buy" or being used as the "product" ourselves to support some social media ad model. Instead, how might we introduce new utility (i.e., functionality) that gives someone a new path to enjoy benefits that they do not experience today? How might we provide the right, curated amounts of information to give people confidence that they should use (and keep using) the utility we just provided them? Finally, if we show up correctly and add significant value, we will have achieved emotional resonance and our offerings will feel like a natural extension of who they are and what they want to do. Those elements working together inform a moment of truth that we should ensure we double down on our efforts to get right. If we do a great job, we can build an entire business around that moment of truth in someone's journey.

As we craft solutions that meet people where they are, we should thoughtfully consider a wide and holistic range of ingredients we can weave together to achieve the most intuitive, empathic outcome. We should challenge ourselves to think more broadly than the typical default of merely focusing on software. Sure, software eats the world, but the world is now biting back to check software's ambitions at the door. We have to ensure we create what's most thoughtfully in tune with our humanity, subordinating software to its appropriate place. At least, it's my hope that we carry forward this conviction. With the advent of digital, there's so many products and services that fail to thoughtfully serve our well-being. Moore's law may continue to steam ahead, but there's a necessary reckoning in which we need to question where all of this is heading. There are individuals like Monika Bielskyte, Timnit Gebru, and Joy Buolamwini, PhD, who are articulating constructive warnings or at least defining ethical boundary conditions to keep the design of software and generative AI behind appropriate guardrails. The human experience can't be fully satiated with code. Personally, my passion for software only goes so far compared to my peers who navigate the tech industry. I see it merely as another enabler, the same way I view many other design ingredients (physical, spatial, services, content, etc.).

As an industrial designer passionate about physical affordances, I'm drawn to luminary designers (Kenya Hara, Naoto Fukasawa, Jasper Morrison, etc.) who figured out how to make extraordinary physical products that are so normal that their utility and embodiment is actually extraordinary because they blend so well into a person's life. While physical things don't immediately command the same return on investment that software might and their longer lead times of creation can feel intimidating, that doesn't mean we shouldn't try to create the right physical affordances to realize an intuitive, holistic, and relevant experience. Creating the most intuitive, empathic solution can be hard, and we should absolutely attempt to take it on. If the vision is clear, we should embrace creating hard things. At the same time, we can't turn a blind eye to the devastating environmental consequences of producing too much physical stuff that ends up in landfills or contaminates our ecosystems. The optimist in me says we can use our multidisciplinary brainpower to create physical affordances that prove themselves sustainable, regenerative, and mindful of mitigating unintended consequences. There should be meaning and thoughtfulness behind any physical design proposal to ensure the affordance is respectful to the bigger picture of stakeholder needs. Our planet Earth is a stakeholder in this respect. Let's use all of these ingredients to deeply tap into what makes us human and considerate to the larger ecology, and design accordingly.

## PUT FLYWHEELS IN MOTION

The ideas within this book will surely face some challenges in the business world due to past precedent and economic headwinds. There are plenty of paradigms that get in the way of our pursuit of innovation, especially as we navigate the forest of ambiguity. It will be a journey, not a sprint. Resistance could range from company politics to a lack of education about design, conventional business precedents, and just a whole lot of baggage across each discipline. Economic challenges can make the resistance worse as it breeds short-term thinking just to survive unfavorable market conditions. However, there are additional things we can do within our teams, approach, and means of empowerment to accelerate our efforts. Think about that flywheel, as the analogous mechanism that smooths out shakes and bumps in any dynamic system. Once you get a flywheel going, it's hard to slow down even in the face of resistance. While we know that realizing innovation represents a mixture of proactiveness and patience, we want to apply some level of acceleration where we can increase the probability of having lightning strike in our favor. What flywheels can you employ to modulate the turbulence to leverage design and the broader multidisciplinary team most effectively in your pursuit of innovation?

As we begin the journey of taking multidisciplinary teams through the nonlinear paces of the creative process, we learn that it's no longer enough to have designers tack sketches and wire-frames up on the wall with no supporting context. If I'm a colleague unfamiliar with design, it's going to be really hard to figure out how to react to what I'm seeing. Incorporating and raising visibility of guiding principles for design alongside the design and product work is critical to getting people on the same page with iterations that are emerging from the team's work. For the next product review, the designer can stand up and defend their deliverables with their "cheat sheet" of notes that speak to the rhyme and reason for every element of their proposed user experience. This proves immensely helpful to minimize anyone in the room feeling like they need to cramp their brains to understand the fundamental logic before they can get to a place to offer helpful, constructive feedback. We've all been there. Guiding principles for design accelerate our momentum to achieve understanding within any room in which we're sitting. They also provide an important opportunity to lend voice to key convictions that break the cycle of being chained to the status quo. This is the case whether it's marketers marketing and consumers consuming, or exploiting people-as-the-product (looking at you, social media), with abrasive conflicts of privacy and our basic human rights. Use guiding principles for design to shine a light on those key convictions where we are tapping into our most humane, ethical, responsible, and thoughtful priorities that have a shot of defeating convention for the sake of realizing something better.

In turn, we can use those guiding principles to effectively compound the turning of another flywheel, which is garnering multidisciplinary feedback. We have to remember that different disciplines have not enjoyed a long precedent of collaborating together in one room. It was always the exception in most organizations, but our present moment and future require it being more of the rule moving forward. Feedback is a tricky thing to navigate, and we definitely want our stakeholders and sponsors spending their time doubling down on the sharp points that matter so that the multidisciplinary team can take their feedback and inform the next steps. Depending on where we are in the creative process, our mindset for feedback has to flex as different situations warrant. As we loosely describe the creative process as being parts divergent ideation and parts convergent ideation, let's be sure to reinforce the necessary contrast of mindsets between the two. In divergence, we want to generate more ideas (and compounding ideas) with less scrutiny. We need an additive mindset that embraces every idea as an interesting thought worth exploring without judgment. "I like that idea, and I also thought of this!" "Yes, and . . .": this is the discussion to have in the team. As we shift to convergence, we ratchet up our discernment and evaluate innovation concepts for their expected impact, the anticipated effort required to build them, and the desirability, business viability, technical feasibility, and strategic alignment required to ensure the proposed solution is worth the investment. We might even have to halt progress on some ideas because they did not pass the evaluation criteria along these dimensions.

Other flywheels include introspection into how we spend our bandwidth as we strive to innovate and incubate intuitive products and services, and how to open our aperture to ensure we're fueled by a diversity of creative inputs to inform new possibilities. On bandwidth, when we think about how full our daily schedules tend to be, we must proactively interrogate where we spend our time. Not everything that claims to be urgent is actually important to bring the best out of us and our capabilities. Assessing importance is the first step, but then we should further categorize of our activities to spot patterns where we are helping or hindering our pursuit of innovation. Typically, we're involved in (1) stakeholder management to keep our stakeholders and sponsors informed and aligned on our plans, (2) production to create deliverables that document our thoughts and arguments as we engage our stakeholders, and (3) creative problem-solving, which involves the deep creative work to fuel innovation. If we care about realizing the most intuitive products and services from our multidisciplinary efforts, then we have to protect the third category at all costs. On sustaining an open aperture, we need to ensure we're always scanning the long-term time horizon for trends and inspirations that can inform opportunities in the short, mid, and long terms. This requires maintaining an open-source approach, exercising our future visioning muscles, and engaging in communities where thought leadership and best practices are constantly shared. No matter how much we're immersed in short-term delivery, we need to have our eyes raised, always looking to put two and two together based on the things we see coming over the future time-horizon.

I saved the last flywheel, the prioritization of DEI, for last. Upon reflection, it's probably a bigger source of momentum than the metaphor of a flywheel can do justice. Our human collective is a beautiful mosaic of difference, a beautiful tapestry of intersectionalities. We are more connected than ever thanks to digital technology. As individuals, we each bring something unique to the world, and we should draw from our lived experience to richly color the perspectives and gifts that we share. At the same time, our own story does not give us the right to assume what's happening with someone else's experiences without including, respecting, and welcoming their voice, their story, and their full humanity. Otherwise, we risk being very wrong. That's why I've said before that I can only speak for me as a Black man navigating corporate America. I can't pretend to speak for the adversity, specific realities, and circumstances of others. What I have noticed in my work is that my Black identity and experience have made my curiosity for marginalized and/or underrepresented experiences even sharper, to where I lean in a bit harder to learn from others compared to my peers from majority demographics. My instincts fire a bit quicker to listen, engage, and co-create with other voices not already part of the team conversation. From my experience, there's a natural proclivity to at least ask, "Who are we leaving out? Who are we missing from this conversation?"

Everyone needs to ask these questions more and more because it's simply the right thing to do and we'll leave a lot on the table if we do not. Otherwise, gaps and mismatches will continue to pervade what brands are delivering. Unmet needs and potential harm will grow, especially as digital and generative AI continue to accelerate our reality. Diversity begets creativity, creativity begets innovation, and innovation begets relevant growth for any type of business. We can realize that growth by cultivating relevant, intuitive innovations and demonstrating meaningful impact with our most important stakeholders. While the human imperative of doing right by each other should be a ubiquitous notion, we still have factions of people that hold onto their fear, ignorance, and all the isms (sexism, racism, ageism, etc.) that plague us. They've contorted their minds to believe that they have to give up power and privilege to placate DEI initiatives—a threat in the face of the benefits of ensuring other voices are included. While these folks may personally benefit by maintaining the status quo or doing harm covertly, these people hold back organizations from their true potential. Their behavior functions like a cancer, rendering organizations unable to reduce their blind spots. Sadly, company leaders may not be incentivized to care as they may be driven to achieve their short-term business metrics, despite the fact that their organization's future potential might be eroding from under their feet due to negative people with corrosive mentalities toward DEI.

I've encountered these people. In recruiting, it's the manager who swiftly dismisses a candidate because their resume doesn't check all the boxes that "feel" right according to their comfort zone and subjective measures of success. No wonder more of the same get hired: "I don't know if I'll 'like' this person or could see having a beer with them after work." What? What are we even talking about that's concrete and objective? In the actual job itself, it's the coworker who's belligerent toward someone who they feel doesn't deserve the role they've been assigned. They feel they've missed out due to a DEI quota and question the other person's merit. They make that person's life harder through terrible, passive aggressive behavior. I've experienced this. I had an office neighbor never follow through on any of my requests, feigning that they always knew better and posting a sign on their wall that implied that everyone around them was stupid. At the same time, management interpreted their belligerence as "leadership" and the signs of a go-getter who could command influence and lead teams forward. Despite the lack of contributions to ever help me, this person was labeled a high-potential leader in the making for such toxic behavior. At the same time, senior leaders would ask me, "Why can't you be more like them?" or would talk about me behind my back, dinging me for not being as aggressive. I was expected to assimilate and swallow my differences to follow behaviors that reinforced harm. No thank you. Sadly, in those moments, I took on the unfair burden to try to navigate around that negativity. It hurt me, and it hurt the company's future potential.

## UNCERTAINTY FROM GENERATIVE AI

A wild card has emerged that posits itself as a potential threat or an accelerant to our ambitions. It's the wild card of generative AI. At one extreme, there are voices such as Geoffrey Hinton (a former Google AI pioneer), who highlighted generative AI as one of the biggest existential threats to mankind: "The idea that this stuff could actually get smarter than people—a few people believed that. But most people thought it was way off. And I thought it was way off. I thought it was 30 to 50 years or even longer away. Obviously, I no longer think that."[3] At the other extreme are folks who are proactively building to unlock the true potential of AI, with personalities like Sam Altman and his team at OpenAI.[4] Somewhere along the spectrum are voices like Timnit Gebru (founder and executive director at the Distributed AI Research Institute) and futurist and speculative designer Monika Bielskyte, who are pointing out the dystopia that's already affecting marginalized communities today and how generative AI could further exacerbate problems if we don't get ahead of it by wiring generative AI with more regulation and ethical guardrails. For me, I am trying my best to treat generative AI like any technology, an enabler that we can steer to serve our intentions. I don't want to fear it (though I'm rightfully concerned and cautious), but I do want to understand it and continue experimenting with it.

At a recent DMI Design Leadership Conference in Cambridge, Massachusetts, we hosted keynote speaker Anat Lechner, PhD, a professor of business management at the New York University Stern School of Business and founder and CEO of Huedata, a color intelligence company that leverages AI.[5] In her talk, she characterized the pace of AI advancement and explored what it could mean for the design profession in the wake of fears that AI could replace designers by automating creative tasks. She didn't foresee a devaluing of creative problem-solving from AI, but encouraged us to contemplate the marriage of data, AI, and design capabilities as necessary to be resonate in the future. In her words, "AI might not replace you, but a person who uses AI will."[6] We also hosted John Maeda for a virtual fireside chat hosted by yours truly. Maeda shared his views on design's place in the emerging AI paradigm. He definitely agreed with Lechner's views and sees design playing a more systematic role in resolving gaps in large language models (LLMs) and informing the vectors of context required for embedding AI within future-state applications. This will be necessary for AI to prove itself useful. Maeda's been openly experimenting with new generative AI platforms in his new show, *Mr. Maeda's Cozy AI Kitchen,* featured on Microsoft's developer-serving YouTube channel.[7] Through experiments, we can foresee AI playing a role throughout many nonlinear steps in the creative journey (quant, qual, divergent ideation, simulation, testing, etc.), especially through the forest of ambiguity in pursuit of multidisciplinary innovation.

*Nonlinear: Navigating Design with Curiosity and Conviction* speaks to creatively curious people who want to instigate meaningful change for the future of business, the future stories we want to realize, and the implications that cascade to hopefully inform a better world. Right now, the world is the way it is by some design, for right, wrong, or indifferent. No matter your discipline, you will find yourself having to understand design in the context of multidisciplinary teaming, now and into the future. Having the right disciplines around the table is the first step, and hopefully the team we see is inclusive and representative of our society's beautiful diversity. That's not enough by itself. How they choose to navigate forward is important too. The right composition of team could easily fall into the trap of following rote, formulaic approaches based on prior business convention. Usually that requires certainty and limited risk-taking. That's not going to breed innovation. Our teams need more freedom, safely, and flexibility to try different ways of problem-solving. In the forest of ambiguity, getting to a point and deciding the next move with the best information you have is the challenge. Then you have to move to the next point and reassess where you are. Sometimes you'll frame your boundary conditions and opportunity spaces; other times you'll investigate or explore along a number of different vectors. You'll ideate some and perhaps loop back to investigating some more. The journey is about taking steps, experimenting, making choices, pivoting, and falling forward to learn what resonates.

In my travels, I'm often asked, "What was your motivation to begin writing books?" When I look back, I found myself in a number of situations where I was in that forest of ambiguity, clambering to find my way and be a part of something that could spark something new. Call it *innovation*. Whether I succeeded or failed in those moments, the important thing was that I learned so much through my trials and tribulations. When there wasn't a playbook, my teams and I had to create one (actually several). I just want the experience to be a bit easier for the next team that comes along with an ambition to innovate. The books I write represent amazing opportunities to crystallize learnings for the benefit of the next generation of brave souls that want to scratch the itch of their curiosity and convictions. With the challenges we all experienced in recent years, my writing surprisingly shifted to embrace my lived experience as the foundation for contextualizing any lessons or frameworks that I could offer. In hindsight, the overt, jarring events of 2020 (e.g., the COVID-19 pandemic, AAPI hate crimes, and George Floyd's murder at the hands of the police) triggered something within me. As I unpacked my multidisciplinary experiences, I couldn't help but connect the overt with the covert resistance (gatekeeping, racism, microaggressions, etc.)

that I remembered experiencing. Something would be missing from my writing if I failed to make that connection. *Nonlinear* comes directly from my lived experience. *Reimagining Design* came directly from my lived experience.

*Nonlinear* shines a light on our unique opportunity to meet our present moment and the needs of our future by leveraging design differently than formulaic convention. When design is positioned as an equal force at the problem-solving table in our efforts to serve a hyperconnected, diverse, converging, and exponentially changing world, powerful things can happen. We need to comprehend design's complexities and nuances as we navigate that forest of ambiguity (see figure 8.1) in pursuit of unlocking meaningful innovation. I believe every teammate (regardless of discipline) needs to make it their requirement to understand the nonlinear advantages design can bring to their team. No matter who you are, you will be sitting next to a designer in your team room more and more, and building an appreciation for the subtleties, the choices, the vectors, and ways to empower creative problem-solving will be paramount as we move forward. My hope is that this book provides some color for you to understand the counterintuitive twists and turns and the complexities that we need to be mindful of if we want our design talent to have a chance to be successful alongside other disciplines in the business world. By doing so, the other disciplines will be more successful by learning to embrace nonlinear choices and design's intuitive ability to help that along.

The leadership tactics necessary to accomplish this will be interesting ones. While the team might appoint a de facto leader to steer the ship, leadership should be shared, like an orchestra balancing its leadership across different musical chairs. There will be areas where the businessperson will spike. There will be areas for the technologist to weigh in on how emerging technology could inspire the journey or how feasible something is to create. The designer will have their approach, and hopefully leverage the courage to be subversive with creative skills to move the business forward. For any of these disciplines to be successful in leading and sharing the leadership burden with each other, they have to avoid mapping themselves to a formulaic leadership precedent in the business world, which doesn't like risk. Each leader has to avoid snapping into an overused alpha archetype of command and control. We have to play to our different strengths, allowing leadership to manifest differently. Shortly after *Reimagining Design: Unlocking Strategic Innovation* launched into the world, John Maeda found himself in Los Angeles, and we took an early morning drive to catch up and talk about the book (see figure 8.2).[8] Maeda made me aware of a term that originated with Margaret Stewart, VP of product design and responsible innovation at Meta, called the *situational extrovert*: "Making is a kind of extroverting," Maeda remarked. He's right. An engineer can lead a team forward to a new vector just by bringing a prototype into the room. A designer can offer a sketch that synthesizes the collective input of the team to provoke what we might create together.

This is the new horizon of leadership opportunity that awaits us. Can we rise to the occasion? I would like to think so. We just have to get comfortable with embracing nonlinearity as a means of navigating to realize meaningful and relevant innovation. "To get something you never had, you have to do something you never

**Figure 8.2**
John Maeda and Kevin Bethune discuss *Reimagining Design: Unlocking Strategic Innovation* while in the car for Maeda's YouTube channel.

did."[9] The future and all of its uncertainty requires this courage from us. To get started, look at yourself in the mirror. Use my writings as a figurative mirror if necessary to help in your reflection. What are you curious about? What gaps and unmet needs continue to bug you as you navigate your journey? Then, interrogate what you've done to this point and how your lived experiences colored your travels. How do your experiences, perspectives, and background potentially influence your ability to shape the future you want? What's missing? How might you go on a quest to renew or reinvent yourself, to equip yourself and position yourself to be a more effective leader, practitioner, and change agent? Just know that the path will not be linear. Your first steps to answer these questions will not be about whether they are right or wrong bets. The secret is to get moving so that you can build momentum to learn as fast as you can. *Fall forward.* Be nonlinear.

## ACKNOWLEDGMENTS

I am truly grateful for the opportunity to share perspectives and convictions that can serve as a mirror for every reader to "see" themselves a little differently through my writings. You have unique talents and you're fully capable. Let's shape a better future, together.

Special thanks to the MIT Press for believing in this project, and for the honor of positioning it within the Simplicity: Design, Business, Technology, Life series. Bob Prior, thank you for your generous wisdom, trust, and encouragement through this nonlinear journey working together for a second time.

John Maeda, thank you for your mentorship, encouragement, and friendship. Thank you for always advocating for the inclusion of new voices, and for opening doors for me ever since I met you in San Francisco.

To the esteemed designers, writers, and multidisciplinary misfits who served as technical reviewers on key arguments, frameworks, and examples—Katherine Bennett, Indi Young, Ellen McGirt, Lubna Ahmad, and Jessica Helfand: thank you for your time, guidance, and profound expertise.

To my mentors, teachers, advocates, encouragers, confidantes, collaborators, and servant leaders—Kevin Carroll, D'Wayne Edwards, Gary Hustwit, Maurice Cherry, Patricia Moore, RitaSue Siegel, Jon Fortt, Tony Norman, Dori Tunstall, Annie Jean-Baptiste, Kat Holmes, Alison Rand, Dana Arnett, Su Mathews Hale, Maria Giudice, Sheryl Cababa, Michael Bierut, Debbie Millman, Steven Heller, the team at DesignObserver, Natalie Nixon, Greg Hoffman, Dantley Davis, Forest Young, Lee Moreau, Hugh Weber (RIP), Mark Rutledge, Tara Robertson, Harrison Wheeler, Ti Chang, Raja Schaar, George Aye, Sarah Brooks, Karel Golta, Ron Clark, Monika Bielskyte, Mark Smith (my "twin brother" in Europe), Gavin Ivester, Ruben Hughes, Josh Itiola, Dawn Moses, Justin McElderry, Malcolm Johnson, the team at Langdon Park Capital, Jonathan Johnsongriffin, Andia Winslow, Fiona Atzler, Jeff Henderson, Anthony Marshall, Kristen Shenk, Helen Walters, Allison Fonder, Lesley-Ann Noel, Mariana Mihalakis, Mauro Porcini, Alfredo Muccino, Becca Wright, Karim Rashid, Ernesto Quinteros, Richard Ting, David Hoang, Sean Klimczak, Paul Rainey, Errol Williams, Mark Tate, Gina Warren, Jason Mayden, Angela Snow, Christopher Williams, Paul Nselel, Julian Duncan, Kris Aman, Sennai Atsbeha, Dario Calmese, Iddris Sandu, Michael Johnson, Sheng-Hung Lee, Zariah Cameron, Jacqui Frey, Miranda Fung, Liliana Becerra, Krystina Castella, Poonacha Machaiah, Jenn Ok, Astor Chambers, Sebastian Gier, Christian Robert, Safir

Bellali, Sofie Calderon Boulad, Jessie Kawata, Matt Iversen, Patty Ross, Ron Lish, Monty Mayko, Mark Allen, Bruce Kilgore, Sandy Bodecker (RIP), Janett Nichol, Eric Sprunk, John Hoke, Leo Saldana, Aki Lendahls, Michael Steen, Aaron Cooper, Ronnie Wright, Nikole Hannah-Jones, Faraji Hannah-Jones, Andrew Nagata, Kisun Kim, Natsai Audrey Chieza, Tabi Bonney, Chris Denson, Nigel Sylvester, Samuel Ashby, Reginald Dulaney, Sola Talabi, Dan Trombola, Sandy Rupprecht, Tony Greco, Don Seeger, Albert Shum, Byron Merritt, Susan Gornell, Rich Lesser, La Mer Walker, H. Wook Kim, Walter Delph, Mike Schwartz, Raj Ganguly. Rob Haywood, my original BCGDV design family, the BCGDV founding team, the team at Pave, Wayne Robins, Ammon Haggerty, Sally Chung, Harnish Jani, Richard Holbrook, Julian Ryder, Lloyd Walker, Andy Ogden, my ArtCenter College of Design family, the ArtCenter Board of Trustees, Karen Hofmann, Lorne Buchman, Tom Cordner, Colleen McMullen, Anijo Mathew, Scott Shim, Hector Silva, Amy O'Keefe, my Northwestern EDI family, the team at Invoy, the team at Keevo, Carole Bilson, my Design Management Institute family, my Focus Takigahara family, my Design Leadership Initiative family, the Design Leaders Community and my Design.Co family: thank you.

To my parents, Lonnie and Beverly Bethune, thank you for your love, sacrifices, and the world you opened up to your kids. To my siblings, Serene and Travis, thank you for your love and unwavering support. To my wife, Sefanit, thank you for being you, always making me laugh, and warming my heart. Ezra, I love you, my son. You make me so proud. Finally, I would like to thank God for the strength, favor, and grace to write another book.

# NOTES

## Chapter 1

1. *Merriam-Webster*, s.v. "vector," accessed November 4, 2023, https://www.merriam-webster.com/dictionary/vector.

2. University of Pennsylvania, "Penn's 2011 Commencement Address by Denzel Washington," YouTube, video, May 16, 2011, 22:35, https://www.youtube.com/watch?v=vpW2sGlCtaE.

3. See the BCG X website at https://www.bcg.com/x.

## Chapter 2

1. The P&L summarizes the roll-up of incoming revenues, the COGS, operating expenses, marketing expenses, miscellaneous expenses that are considered "other," interest (either interest paid or interest received), and taxes to yield a final picture of net income or profitability over a given

period. Earnings before interest, tax, depreciation, and amortization (EBITDA) tends to be the highlighted financial metric that isolates the apples-to-apples profitability of the company by excluding those one-off factors that add noise to the underlying story of true profitability over different periods of time.

The balance sheet represents a living accumulation of the business value of an entity. There are two sides to a balance sheet. On the left side, its line items track the amount of assets (cash, receivables, property, goodwill, etc.) an entity has accumulated. The right side of the balance sheet informs a sense of perceived value. On this side, there are two primary categories (liabilities and equity) that, when combined, must equal the same amount as the left side, or assets. This equal state is what gives the balance sheet its name.

The cash flow statement tracks the flow of actual cash between operating, investing, and/or financing activities.

2.  See the Survey Monkey website at https://www.surveymonkey.com/.

3.  Michael E. Porter, "How Competitive Forces Shape Strategy," *Harvard Business Review* 57, no. 2 (May 1979): 137–145.

## Chapter 3

1. Katherine Bennett, in a Zoom call with Kevin Bethune on August 16, 2022, reflected on the untapped potential for design investigative research to unearth meaningful, qualitative insights.

2. Elizabeth B.-N. Sanders, "Design Research in 2006," *Design Research Quarterly* 1, no. 1 (September 2006), https://maketools.com/downloads.

3. See the Invoy website at https://www.invoy.com.

4. Lubna Ahmad, in a Zoom call with Kevin Bethune on August 1, 2023, reflected on the working relationship between Invoy and dreams • design + life.

5. Katherine Bennett, "Designing Design Research," *Design Investigations* (blog), September 28, 2009, http://www.designinvestigations.com/blog /month/september-2009.

6. Anton Nikolov, "Design Principle: Root of the Problem," Medium, UX Planet, March 11, 2017, https://uxplanet.org/design-principles-root-of -the-problem-33899991c9e50.

7. Ahmad, Zoom call with Bethune, August 1, 2023.

8. Affinity mapping is the process of organizing granular observations to eventually uncover latent insights, network effects, and patterns.

9. Bennett, Zoom call with Bethune, August 16, 2022.

10. Indi Young, *Time to Listen: How Giving People Space to Speak Drives Invention and Inclusion* (San Francisco: Indi Young Books, 2022.

11. Indi Young, in a Zoom call with Kevin Bethune on October 4, 2022, discussed her latest views on qualitative investigation within design and innovation projects.

## Chapter 4

1. Jonathan Ball, "The Double Diamond: A Universally Accepted Depiction of the Design Process," Design Council, October 1, 2019, https:// www.designcouncil.org.uk/our-work/news-opinion/double-diamond -universally-accepted-depiction-design-process/.

2. Vijay Kumar and Patrick Whitney, "Daily Life, Not Markets: Customer-Centered Design," *Journal of Business Strategy* 28, no. 4 (2007): 46–58, https://doi.org/10.1108/02756660710760944.

3. See the Keevo Hardware Wallet website at https://www.keevowallet.com/.

4. A market funnel is a journey-based representation of the buying steps of customer awareness, consideration, conversion, and follow-on retention or loyalty to keep customers coming back for future purchases.

5. Joseph Campbell, *The Hero with a Thousand Faces* (Novato, CA: New World Library, 2018).

6. Rikke Dam and Teo Siang, "From Prototype to Product: Ensure That Your Solution Is Feasible and Viable," Interaction Design Foundation, May 2, 2022, https://www.interaction-design.org/literature/article/from -prototype-to-product-ensuring-your-solution-is-feasible-and-viable.

## Chapter 5

1. See dreams • design + life, "Conversation with John Maeda and Kevin Bethune," YouTube, video, June 11, 2020, 35:10, https://www.youtube.com /watch?v=99WNvogLBzQ.

2. Pamela B. Rutledge, "Social Networks: What Maslow Misses," *Psychology Today*, November 8, 2011, https://www.psychologytoday.com/us/blog /positively-media/201111/social-networks-what-maslow-misses-0#:~:text =But%20here's%20the%20problem%20with,collaboration%2C%20 there%20is%20no%20survival.

3. BCG Digital Ventures – Part of BCG X, "DV Alumni: Talking AI-Powered Offer Automation with Christian Selchau-Hansen, CEO of Formation," Medium, September 14, 2020, https://medium.com/bcg-digital -ventures/dv-alumni-talking-ai-powered-marketing-automation-with- christian-selchau-hansen-ceo-of-formation-698ea0f423f6.

4. Greg Hoffman, *Emotion by Design: Creative Leadership Lessons from a Life at Nike* (New York: Twelve / Hachette Book Group, 2022).

5. Hoffman, *Emotion by Design*, 212.

## Chapter 6

1. Marc Andreessen, "Why Software Is Eating the World," Andreessen Horowitz, August 20, 2011, https://a16z.com/2011/08/20/why-software-is -eating-the-world/.

2. Kenya Hara, *Designing Design* (Baden, Switzerland: Lars Müller Publishers, 2014).

3. Naoto Fukasawa and Jasper Morrison, *Super Normal: Sensations of the Ordinary* (Baden, Switzerland: Lars Müller Publishers, 2007).

4. See the Rabbit website at https://www.rabbit.tech/.

5. Keevo, "Keevo Design with Kevin Bethune," YouTube, video, February 11, 2020, 4:14, https://www.youtube.com/watch?v=XmvHk9vBeC4&t =86s.

6. Jessica Helfand, *Design: The Invention of Desire* (New Haven, CT: Yale University Press, 2016), 24.

### Chapter 7

1. Jim Collins, *Good to Great: Why Some Companies Make the Leap . . . and Others Don't* (New York: HarperCollins, 2001).

2. See the Miro website at https://www.miro.com/.

3. See the Japan House Los Angeles website at https://www.japanhousela .com/.

4. See the Design Management Institute website at https://www.dmi.org.

5. Nicole Gull McElroy, "Designing the Change: Black Designers on Equity and Representation in the Industry," *Fortune*, February 15, 2022, https:// fortune.com/2022/02/15/black-designers-on-equity-and-representation-in -the-industry/.

6. David Heinemeier Hansson, "The Waning Days of DEI's Dominance," Hey, November 21, 2022, https://world.hey.com/dhh/the-waning-days-of -dei-s-dominance-9a5b656c.

7. Mauro Porcini, *The Human Side of Innovation: The Power of People in Love with People* (Oakland, CA: Berrett-Koehler Publishers, 2023).

## Chapter 8

1. Mark Wilson, "Design Giant IDEO Cuts a Third of Staff and Closes Offices as the Era of Design Thinking Ends," *Fast Company*, November 3, 2023, https://www.fastcompany.com/90976682/design-giant-ideo-cuts-a-third-of-staff-and-closes-offices-as-the-era-of-design-thinking-ends.

2. Katherine Bennett, in a Zoom call with Kevin Bethune on August 16, 2022, reflected on the untapped potential for design investigative research to unearth meaningful, qualitative insights.

3. Cade Metz, "'The Godfather of A.I.' Leaves Google and Warns of Danger Ahead," *New York Times*, May 4, 2023.

4. See the OpenAI website at https://openai.com/.

5. See the Huedata website at https://www.hue-data.com.

6. Anat Lechner, "What's Next: AI, Analytics and the Coming Transformation of Design," keynote lecture, DMI Design Leadership Conference, Cambridge, MA, September 26, 2023.

7. Microsoft Developer, "Mr. Maeda's Cozy AI Kitchen Coming in October," YouTube, video, September 26, 2023, 0:49, https://www.youtube.com/watch?v=wi-5fhJyrMo.

8. John Maeda: Design & AI, "Driving with Kevin Bethune, Author of Reimagining Design," YouTube, video, April 3, 2022, 8:20, https://www.youtube.com/watch?v=zwOPL8SXT_g.

9. University of Pennsylvania, "Penn's 2011 Commencement Address by Denzel Washington," YouTube, video, May 16, 2011, 22:35, https://www.youtube.com/watch?v=vpW2sGlCtaE.

SUGGESTED READING

Chapter 1: Zig Then Zag

Bethune, Kevin. *Reimagining Design: Unlocking Strategic Innovation.* Cambridge, MA: MIT Press, 2022.

Fayard, Anne-Laure, and Sarah Fathallah. "Design Thinking Misses the Mark." *Stanford Social Innovation Review* 22, no. 1 (Winter 2024): 28–35. https://ssir.org/articles/entry/design_thinking_misses_the_mark#.

Berry, Anne H., Kareem Collie, Penina Acayo Laker, Lesley-Ann Noel, Jennifer Rittner, and Kelly Walters. *The Black Experience in Design: Identity, Expression and Reflection.* New York: Allworth Press 2022.

MacKenzie, Gordan. *Orbiting the Giant Hairball: A Corporate Fool's Guide to Surviving with Grace.* New York: Viking Penguin, 1998.

Carroll, Kevin. *Rules of the Red Rubber Ball: Find and Sustain Your Life's Work.* New York: ESPN Books, 2004.

Bethune, Kevin. "What Nike Taught Me about Collaborative Design." *Fast Company*, March 9, 2022. https://www.fastcompany.com/90729494/what-nike-taught-me-about-collaborative-design.

Bethune, Kevin. "The 4 Superpowers of Design." Filmed October 2017 in Milan. TED video, 12:57. https://www.ted.com/talks/kevin_bethune_the_4_superpowers_of_design.

BCG Digital Ventures—Part of BCG X. "DV Alumni: Unlocking Strategic Innovation with Design Visionary, Kevin Bethune." Medium, BCG Digital Ventures, May 25, 2022. https://medium.com/bcg-digital-ventures/dv-alumni-unlocking-strategic-innovation-with-design-visionary-kevin-bethune-84bf7d9f6d8b.

### Chapter 2: Quantitative Framing

Martin, Roger. *The Design of Business: Why Design Thinking is the Next Competitive Advantage.* Boston: Harvard Business Review Press, 2009.

Kim, W. Chan, and Renée Mauborgne. *Blue Ocean Strategy: How to Create Uncontested Market Space and Make the Competition Irrelevant.* Boston: Harvard Business Review Press, 2005.

Strategyzer. "The Business Model Canvas." Strategyzer, February 26, 2024. https://www.strategyzer.com/canvas/business-model-canvas.

Walmsley, Craig. "Introducing the Impact Canvas." Medium, October 17, 2019. https://medium.com/@craig_walmsley/introducing-the-impact-canvas-2138433c1eef.

### Chapter 3: Qualitative Design Investigation

Young, Indi. "Archetypes Don't Have Photos, but Characters Do," Medium, Inclusive Software, May 4, 2023. https://medium.com/inclusive-software/archetypes-dont-have-photos-but-characters-do-920a744a2841.

Sanders, Elizabeth B.-N., and Pieter Jan Stappers. *Convivial Toolbox: Generative Research for the Front End of Design*. Amsterdam: BIS Publishers, 2012.

Sanders, Liz, and Pieter Jan Stappers, "From Designing to Co-designing to Collective Dreaming: Three Slices in Time," *Interactions* 21, no. 6 (2014): 24–33. https://doi.org/10.1145/2670616.

Chipchase, Jan, with Simon Steinhardt. *Hidden in Plain Sight: How to Create Extraordinary Products for Tomorrow's Customers*. New York: HarperCollins, 2013.

Zeisel, John. *Inquiry by Design: Environment / Behavior / Neuroscience in Architecture, Interiors, Landscape, and Planning*. New York: W. W. Norton & Company, 2006.

## Chapter 4: Design Ideation

Kumar, Vijay. *101 Design Methods: A Structured Approach for Driving Innovation in Your Organization*. Hoboken, NJ: John Wiley & Sons, 2013.

LUMA Institute. *Innovating for People: Handbook of Human-Centered Design Methods*. Pittsburgh: LUMA Institute, 2012.

Cababa, Sheryl. *Closing the Loop: Systems Thinking for Designers*. New York: Rosenfeld Media, 2023.

## Chapter 5: Designing Moments of Truth

Maeda, John. *How to Speak Machine: Computational Thinking for the Rest of Us*. London: Portfolio/Penguin, 2019.

Hustwit, Gary, dir. *RAMS*. Documentary, 2018. https://hustwit.vhx.tv/.

## Chapter 6: Design Ingredients

Fadell, Tony. *Build: An Unorthodox Guide to Making Things Worth Making*. New York: HarperCollins, 2022.

Hara, Kenya. *Ex-formation*. Zurich: Lars Müller Publishers, 2015.

Hara, Kenya. *White*. Zurich: Lars Müller Publishers, 2010.

Sterling, Bruce. *Shaping Things*. Cambridge, MA: MIT Press, 2005.

Tuck, Andrew, ed. *The Monocle Guide to Good Business*. Berlin: Gestalten, 2014.

## Chapter 7: Flywheel Effects

Nixon, Natalie. *The Creativity Leap: Unleash Curiosity, Improvisation, and Intuition at Work*. Oakland, CA: Berritt-Koehler Publishers, 2020.

BCG Digital Ventures—Part of BCG X. "Reimagining Design: 5 Takeaways from a Conversation with Innovation Leader, Kevin Bethune." Medium, BCG Digital Ventures, June 9, 2022. https://medium.com/bcg-digital-ventures/reimagining-design-5-takeaways-from-a-conversation-with-innovation-leader-kevin-bethune-a753c4fe5b12.

## Chapter 8: Final Thoughts

Heller, Steven. "The Daily Heller: Realism Plus Dreams Equals Reimagined Design." *Print Magazine*, March 9, 2022. https://www.printmag.com/daily-heller/the-daily-heller-designers-meet-the-imaginers/.

Buchman, Lorne M. *Make to Know: From Spaces of Uncertainty to Creative Discovery*. New York: Thames & Hudson, 2021.

Holmes, Kat. *Mismatch: How Inclusion Shapes Design*. Cambridge, MA: MIT Press, 2018.

Tunstall, Elizabeth (Dori). *Decolonizing Design: A Cultural Justice Guidebook*. Cambridge, MA: MIT Press, 2023.

Bielskyte, Monika. "Protopia Futures [Framework]." Medium, Protopia Futures, May 18, 2021. https://medium.com/protopia-futures/protopia-futures-framework-f3c2a5d09a1e.

Buolamwini, Joy. *Unmasking AI: My Mission to Protect What Is Human in a World of Machines.* New York: Random House, 2023.

Golta, Karel J., Eva Simone Lihotzky, Shannon Mullen O'Keefe, Adriana C. M. Nugter, and Winnie So. *10 Moral Questions: How to Design Tech and AI Responsibly.* Q Collective, 2024.

Rubin, Rick. *The Creative Act: A Way of Being.* New York: Penguin Press, 2023.

Mayden, Jason. *The Speed of Grace.* Los Angeles: Trillicon Valley, 2023.

Bethune, Kevin. "Servant Leaders and Gatekeepers." *Design Management Review* 30 (2019): 14–15. https://doi.org/10.1111/drev.12190.

Bethune, Kevin, and Andia Winslow. "A Beautiful Future." YouTube, video, February 4, 2019, 1:26. https://www.youtube.com/watch?v=jdehRIib5uA &t=1s.

# INDEX

Trend curation, 33
Trends, 20, 24, 26, 33, 52, 70,
    93–94, 99–100, 146, 159, 161–
    162, 191
Trombola, Dan, 175
Tunstall, Dori, 152
Twitter, 109, 169. *See also* X

Uber, 48, 113, 131
UK Design Council, 82
Unintended consequences, 77
United Kingdom, 113
University of Notre Dame, 11
University of Pennsylvania, 8,
    88, 183
Utility, 114, 117, 126, 137, 142, 186

Value criteria, 77, 92, 118
Vector, 7–8, 51, 58, 60–61, 70, 79,
    86–88, 110, 125, 181, 199
Vitsœ, 113, 137

Wall Street, 3, 39, 178
*Wall Street Journal*, 33
Washington, Denzel, 8, 88, 183
Wavelength, 89–90
Weight-management, 57–58, 63–
    64, 120, 122
Westinghouse Electric Company,
    12, 138, 175
Woke, 168

X, 109. *See also* Twitter

Yamaha Motor Company, 74
Young, Indi, 74, 76
YouTube, 139, 196, 200

Zeisel, John, 54
Zoom, 2, 21, 54, 58